GOLF

101 WINNING GOLF TIPS

2nd Edition

Also by John Andrisani

101 Supershots (with Chi Chi Rodriguez)
A-Game Golf (with John Anselmo)
The Bobby Jones Way
Complete Idiot's Guide to Improving Your Short Game (with Jim McLean)
Everything I Learned About People, I Learned from a Round of Golf
The Four Cornerstones of Winning Golf (with Butch Harmon)
The Golf Doctor (with Robin McMillan)
Golf Heaven
GOLF Magazine's Complete Book of Golf Instruction (with George Peper, Jim
Frank, and Lorin Anderson)
Golf Rules Plain and Simple (with Mark Russell)
Golf Your Way (with Phil Ritson)
Grip It and Rip It! (with John Daly)
Hit It Hard! (with Mike Dunaway)
The Hogan Way
The Killer Swing (with John Daly)
Learning Golf: The Lyle Way (with Sandy Lyle)
The Michelle Wie Way
Natural Golf (with Seve Ballesteros)
The Nicklaus Way
The Plane Truth for Golfers (with Jim Hardy)
The Plane Truth for Golfers Master Class (with Jim Hardy)
Play Golf the Tiger Woods Way
Play Like Sergio Garcia
Playing Lessons (with Butch Harmon)
The Short Game Magic of Tiger Woods
SuperGolf
Think Like Tiger
The Tiger Woods Way
Tiger's New Swing
Total Golf (with Phil Ritson)
Total Shotmaking (with Fred Couples)
The X-Factor (with Jim McLean)

GOLFWEEK'S
101 WINNING
GOLF TIPS
2nd Edition

Become a shot-making virtuoso with Tips
from the Tour's Top Pros

John Andrisani

SKYHORSE PUBLISHING

Skyhorse Publishing books may be purchased in bulk at special discounts for
sales promotion, corporate gifts, fund-raising, or educational purposes. Special
editions can also be created to specifications. For details, contact the Special
Sales Department, Skyhorse Publishing, 307 West 36th Street, 11th Floor, New
York, NY 10018 or info@skyhorsepublishing.com.

www.skyhorsepublishing.com

10 9 8 7 6 5 4 3 2 1

2nd Edition ISBN: 978-1-61608-200-0

Library of Congress Cataloging-in-Publication Data

Andrisani, John.
Golfweek's 101 winning golf tips / John Andrisani.
p. cm.
Includes index.
ISBN-13: 978–1–60239–016–4 (pbk. : alk. paper)
ISBN-10: 1–60239–016–9 (pbk. : alk. paper)
1. Golf. I. Golf magazine. II. Title. III. Title: Golfweek's one hundred one
winning
golf tips. IV. Title: 101 winning golf tips.
GV965.A565 2007
796.352—dc22
2007004777

Printed in China

Contents

Introduction

The game of golf is played on courses around the country that, though finely manicured, are anything but perfect, especially when compared to the other settings where other sports, such as basketball, bowling, and billiards are played. Typically, on public and private courses, tees are not perfectly flat, fairways are rolling in spots, and greens often feature two tiers or subtle undulations. Then, of course, there are water hazards, bunkers, trees, and rough.

Granted, on par-4 and par-5 holes, you get to tee the ball up when driving. Still, holes usually curve left or right, so you need to work the ball around the corner of a dogleg. And, if you do hit the ideal shaped tee shot, for example a draw, you still have to hit an exacting approach shot the right distance and in the right direction to land the ball on the green and avoid trouble.

Short par-3 holes demand even more precision, because greens are usually smaller. Therefore, if you choose the wrong club, steer the swing instead of employing a tension free action, or hit the wrong shot, you are going to face a challenging pitch, chip, or sand shot to put the ball in position to save par.

I think Ben Hogan was right to relate one's handicap to the number of errors the player makes during a round. Nowadays, the majority of club-level recreational golfers shoot in the 90s on a par-72 course, so obviously they make a high number of shot-making errors. The irony is that the average golfer is not totally at fault. I say that because I believe there is misinformation being passed on to recreational golfers by teachers across the country. More importantly, golf instructors do exactly what the great teacher and 1948 Masters champion Claude Harmon, Sr. said a teacher should never do: "Teach swing instead of teaching golf."

Claude Harmon knew what his son Butch Harmon (former teacher of Tiger Woods) and other great instructors, as well as great players, know: To become good at golf and shoot good scores, you must be able to hit a wide variety of tee-to-green shots that require setting up and swinging differently than you normally are accustomed to doing.

It's my hope that the 101 shots showcased in this book will help you reach your goal of becoming a shot-making virtuoso; a player who is able to handle any course situation you are confronted with for your golfing lifetime.

John Andrisani
December 2006
Gulfport, Florida

Driving the Ball

The key objective on par-4 and par-5 holes is hitting the fairway, yet course-design features and weather conditions require you to play creative shots to land the ball in scoring position

The first shot played on either a par-4 or par-5 hole, off a tee and between two markers placed several yards apart on an area of manicured grass called the tee-box, is the drive. The purpose of the drive is to hit the ball within a strip of short grass called the fairway, running all the way from the tee to green, ideally in an area that allows you to hit an attacking shot into the green.

The legendary golfer Ben Hogan once said, "If you can't drive the ball, you can't play golf," as if talking to the majority of players who struggle with this department

2

Fred Funk, one of the world's best golfers at hitting controlled drives.

of the game, often slicing drives into trees, water, or rough bordering the fairway.

Ironically, I believe one reason average golfers fail to hit a high number of drives on to the "short grass" during a round of golf has less to do with a lack of talent and more to do with a lack of knowledge regarding how to properly set up to the ball. Let me explain.

When driving, many amateur golfers fail to sweep the ball cleanly off a tee and powerfully into the air because they address the ball in the same way they do when setting up to play a short iron club. Rather than playing out of a wide stance that will provide a strong foundation for swinging the driver (the longest club in the bag with an average length of forty-six inches), middle and high handicap players, in contrast to Ben Hogan in days gone by and Tiger Woods today, spread their feet narrowly apart when addressing the ball. Furthermore, many club-level players set up with their arms hanging straight down instead of extending them outward to feel a strong sense of relaxed tension as they reach for the ball. Consequently, due to incorrect pre-swing preparation, the player is set up to swing the club on a steep plane ideal for a wedge rather than a flat plane ideal for a driver, particularly if the objective is to hit a controlled draw shot.

The driver setup determines, to a large degree, the type of swing you will employ and the type of shot you will hit. So never take the address for granted.

3

Professional golfers and low handicap players know that in order to hit solid, accurate drives a set of basic fundamentals must be heeded. Of course, as you will learn, setup positions change according to the type of driver shot you intend to hit. Having said that, to hit the ball even halfway decently off the tee with the driver, you need, when taking your address, to fall within certain parameters, or what my friend and top-ranked teacher calls "corridors of success." To do that, I recommend that you:

1. Play the ball approximately opposite your left heel in a stance that is a few inches wider than shoulder width.
2. Position your feet, knees, hips, and shoulders parallel to the target line.
3. Set the clubface perpendicular to an area of fairway that you have designated as your target.
4. Point the toe-end of your left foot about 25 degrees away from the target line, and position your right foot almost perpendicular to the target line.
5. Bend comfortably at the knees and waist.
6. Balance your weight evenly between your feet or place about fifty-five percent of it on your right foot.
7. Set up with your left arm and the club-shaft forming a straight line.
8. Position your hands in line with the ball or slightly ahead of the clubhead.

The other reason so many weekend golfers hit a high percentage of weak, off-line drives is they swing the club too fast and off track during the takeaway or initial stage of the swing.

The takeaway is the engine room of the swing. If the initial move you make away from the ball is incorrect, it is highly unlikely that you will be able to swing the club back along the proper path and plane and achieve your ultimate goal—the one all golfers strive for—square club-face-to-ball contact at impact. Frankly, the only way to bail out a bad start to the swing is to reroute the club back on track by jerking it. If you do that, however, you'll likely destroy your natural tempo and rhythm and, at best, hit a drive that finishes in the first cut of rough.

Make no mistake, even veteran players who have the ability to sense an early error in their takeaway can rarely correct it in time to save the swing and hit the good shot they intended. The reason: The entire golf swing takes less than two seconds, from the time you trigger the backswing until the time the ball is struck. Therefore, our reflexes cannot react quickly enough to redirect a faulty start to the swing.

Tiger Woods, like other golfing greats, employs a smooth, evenly paced takeaway action. That's because any good driver of the ball knows that a slow, smooth takeaway is the critical link to creating a strong coiling action of the body and a full weight shift onto the right side in the backswing—two keys to swinging the club power-fully into the back of the ball with the sweet spot of the clubface finishing dead square to the target.

In addition to the vital importance of setting up correctly and employing a deliberate on-path, on-plane takeaway, the other links to good driving involve sticking to a step-by-step pre-swing routine and thinking out each shot strategically.

Whereas the typical amateur rushes the pre-swing routine, the typical tour professional:

1. Stands behind the ball (club in right hand, usually), looking closely at the shape of the hole, checking out hazards, and picking out an area of fairway to land the ball and be in position to hit the most aggressive approach shot.
2. Stares at the target and "sees" the ball flying toward it.
3. Employs one or two practice swings to relax the muscles and rehearse the ideal driver-swing.
4. Walks up to the ball from the side, placing the right foot in the basic position for a driver stance and placing the club squarely behind the ball.
5. Sets the left foot down and, practically simultaneously, jockeys the body into position while completing the grip and getting the pressure in both hands right; around 6 on a 1–10 scale.

6. Looks back and forth from the ball to the target, two to three times.

Depending on what type of shot the PGA pro intends to hit, he tees the ball up in a different area of the tee-box— *not* midway between the markers as most recreational golfers do nearly all of the time. For example, when playing a right-to-left draw, the professional tees the ball up on the left side of the tee and aims down the right side of the fairway, on the line the ball will fly before curving left toward the center of the fairway.

I know this may sound like a heck of a lot of preparation for just one shot, but not if you consider these truisms:

1. The driver is the club most often used off the tee on par-4 and par-5 holes.
2. Hitting a good drive, especially on the opening hole, raises your level of confidence and relaxes you.
3. Good drives set up good scoring opportunities.

Powerfully hit, accurate drives that fly high and far in the air are certainly a plus on dead-straight par-4 and par-5 holes, particularly on a course featuring lush fairways. However, PGA Tour professionals and low handicap players know from experience that during a round of eighteen holes, different holes require different type drives. For example, on a hole that curves left, you're best served by hitting a draw around the dogleg since this shape of drive

7

essentially shortens the hole and leaves you a shot into the green with a short or medium iron, and these clubs are far easier to hit than a less-lofted long iron or fairway metal club.

Weather conditions and the contour of the fairway are variables that also influence your choice of drive. When hitting into a strong wind, a low shot is required. When hitting to a fairway that is fast-running, and a water-hazard or cross-bunker is within reach, an extra high drive hit with a number-3 fairway metal is the ideal shot. The reason: The ball will land softly on the fairway, short of any hazards. I could go on listing course situations that require different types of drives, but surely you get my point. So let's go to the lesson tee and learn how to play an array of drives so that you can give yourself the best chance of hitting the ball in the best scoring position on the short grass.

◯ *SHOT 1: Dead-Straight Power-Play*

Situation: You are coming down the final hole tied with your match-play opponent. He's a powerful hitter.

Strategy: When all is on the line, you can put yourself on par with a more powerful hitter by employing the following method that will allow you to hit drives twenty yards longer.

8

Shot-Technique Tip: At address, visualize the ball zooming off the clubface and flying down the fairway. Focus on the back center portion of the ball, precisely on the spot where you want the clubface's sweet spot to make contact. Tilt your left hip up higher than your right and make sure your left shoulder is higher than your left. Both of these setup adjustments will allow you to put slightly more weight on your right foot and leg so that, ultimately, you are poised to make a powerful upswing hit at impact.

Extend the club back longer in the takeaway, about eighteen inches, to create a wider and more powerful swing arc. Let your left heel come up off the ground to help you make a stronger body turn and longer swing. Stop swinging when the club reaches a position at the top with the club shaft parallel to the target line and the clubface is in a dead-square position. This will ensure that your club is square to the target, where it needs to be to hit a dead-straight shot.

Tailoring the Tip: There is no better model for learning this shot than Tom Watson, one of golf's all-time great players and a pro I could watch hit drives for hours.

On the downswing, replant your left heel on the ground to trigger a strong leverage action that, in turn, will allow your arms and hands to swing the club squarely into the ball at a higher speed—two ingredients for hitting an on-line power drive.

9

Two reasons why golf legend Tom Watson is such a powerfully accurate driver of the ball is that he stares intently at the target, visualizing the perfect shot before starting the swing (top), and releases the club directly at the target through the impact zone (bottom).

○ SHOT 2: Super-Controlled Power-Slice

Situation: You face a tee shot on a long, very sharp, dog-leg-right, par-4 hole.

Strategy: This hole is so long that you need to cut the dogleg, as good golfers say, by turning the ball sharply around the corner.

Shot-Technique Tip: In preparing to hit this shot, follow this shot-making recipe shared with me by legendary golfer Lee Trevino.

Tee the ball low, take a narrow open stance with your right foot perpendicular to the target line instead of fanned out slightly like your left foot, play the ball off your left instep, weaken your grip by turning both hands toward the target, and position your hands higher and closer to your body.

> **Tailoring the Tip:** For you left-handed golfers who are looking to learn how to hit a controlled slice, the ideal pro-model is Phil Mickelson.

Swing the club back well outside the target line and up to the three-quarter position.

Swing the club down across the target line to impart a high degree of slice-spin on the ball.

○ SHOT 3: Super-Controlled Power-Hook

Situation: You face a tee shot on a long, very sharp, dog-leg-left, par-4 hole.

Strategy: You need to hit a roundhouse hook shot around the dogleg, so that, in effect, you shorten the hole. Here's what the late trick-shot artist Paul Hahn taught me about the ins and outs of playing this shot successfully.

Shot-Technique Tip: At address, tee the ball high, take a wide stance, stand farther from the ball, fan your right foot outward away from the target line, play the ball an inch behind your left heel, strengthen your grip by turning your hands away from the target, position your hands lower and farther from the ball than normal, and turn the clubface inward so that its toe is slightly ahead of its heel.

Swing the club back on a very flat plane and path, up to the parallel position.

Swing the club out toward the ball at the start of the downswing, while rotating your hips counterclockwise and rotating your right hand over (rather than under) your left hand. This unique release action will cause the clubface to close dramatically, allowing you to impart heavy hook-spin on the ball.

> **Tailoring the Tip:** Arnold Palmer is one golfing legend who played this shot to perfection, throughout his long career, particularly during the 1950s and early '60s.
>
> Sergio Garcia is my pick among the "young guns" on the PGA Tour as the best power-hook player.

12

Sergio Garcia's fluid hands-club release action allows him to turn the golf ball powerfully around the corner of sharp curving dogleg left holes.

13

○ SHOT 4: RIDE THE WIND TEE-BALL

Situation: You are on the tee of a par-5 hole, with a wide open fairway in front of you. A strong wind is at your back.

Strategy: You know if you can somehow find a way to take advantage of the wind, you can hit an extra-long drive, reach the green in two shots, and putt for eagle. Here's how to hit a tee-ball that rides the wind—Fred Couples style.

Shot-Technique Tip: At address, play the ball forward in your stance, directly opposite your left toe. Set your hands and head behind the ball.

Make a relaxed upright backswing action, letting your wrists hinge quite early in the takeaway.

On the downswing, keep your head behind the ball. In the hitting area, turn your right hand under your left to help you drive the club and ball up higher into the air.

○ SHOT 5: WIND CHEATER

Situation: You are playing golf on a very windy course, and a headwind is in your face when you stand on the tee.

Strategy: To hit a low, wind-cheater. The best way to accomplish this is to copy the following technique employed by Scottish pro Colin Montgomerie, as well as Tour professionals who grew up in Texas, most notably two time Masters winner Ben Crenshaw.

Shot-Technique Tip: Build a tee by digging the heel of your shoe into the ground. Next, set the ball on the mound of grass that protrudes upward, so a few blades of grass lie between the ball and the clubface.

Swing your number-3 fairway metal club normally. Because grass will fill the grooves on the club, the ball will fly faster off the clubface, cheat the wind, and finish well down the fairway.

○ SHOT 6: SUPER-CONTROLLED DRAW-PLAY

Situation: You face a tee shot on a short par-4 hole that curves or doglegs a little left.

Strategy: Play this shot with a driver if the fairway is wide. However, on a narrow hole, it's best to hit a slight right-to-left draw with a 3-metal fairway club; namely because you could hit a driver shot through the right side of the fairway and knock the ball into trees, rough, or water.

Shot-Technique Tip: Aim the clubface at an area of fairway approximately ten yards right of where you want the ball to land. Relax your grip; "soft" hands will promote a rhythmic backswing and enhance your delivery action on the downswing.

Tailoring the Tip: Judging from the old films I've watched, Bobby Jones was one heck of a draw-player.

These days, statistics show that Fred Funk is one of golf's leading drivers. He can hit the ball dead straight off the tee or pick up extra yards by hitting a hot, controlled draw.

15

Swing the club back inside the target line and up to the three-quarter position.

Trigger the down-motion by nudging your body-weight toward the target and, almost at the same time, drop your right elbow downward toward your right hip to promote a shallow downswing path. Next, release your hands, arms, and club more freely than normal, so that the clubface closes enough at impact to turn the ball left as desired.

○ *SHOT 7: THREE-METAL-FADE*

Situation: You face a tee shot on a short par-4 hole that curves or doglegs a little right.

Strategy: It's best to hit a slight left-to-right fade with a three-metal club, since you could hit a straight drive through the left side of the fairway and land the ball in trouble.

Shot-Technique Tip: PGA Tour veteran Corey Pavin hits this shot (even with the driver) on command, so it's only natural that I advise you to learn the following technique this former U.S. Open winner relayed to me while I worked on a *Golf Magazine* article with him in the mid-1980s.

Aim your feet and body to the left of target, in a slightly open position, at a point where you want the ball to start its flight. Set the clubface down perpendicular to your final target, the area of fairway where you want the ball to land.

Fred Funk's inside take-away action (top) and shallow downswing path (bottom) allow him to hit super-controlled drives.

Swing the club back parallel to your open bodyline, stopping at the three-quarter point.

Swing the club down along your bodyline, so you get the feeling that the club is moving on an out-to-in path.

○ *SHOT 8: SUPER-HOT TWO-IRON STINGER*

Situation: You face a tee-shot on a very narrow par-4, with all kinds of trouble bordering the fairway.

Strategy: It's not worth risking hitting the driver or even a fairway club. So use the 2-iron to your advantage, by putting some sting into the shot the way Tiger Woods does.

Shot-Technique Tip: Tee the ball very low. Grip the club firmly with your left hand, since it is most responsible for controlling the movement of the clubhead. Hold the club more lightly with your right hand, since this grip will allow you to increase your hand-arm speed and add power to your shot. Hood the club so that its face points at the target, but downward slightly.

Swing the club back along a flat path, all the way to the parallel position, with your right wrist hinged slightly.

Tailoring the Tip: Ben Hogan was the best ever at playing this shot, according to many golf experts I spoke to and based on what I learned from studying sequence photographs and illustrations showcasing his unique swing.

18

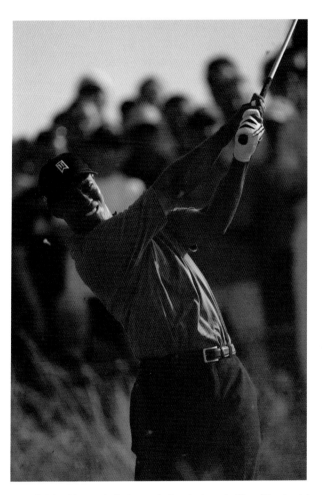

Trying to finish with your belly button facing the target—Tiger Woods style—will encourage you to hit a powerful stinger-shot.

Swing down, delaying the re-hinging of your right wrist until impact, when you should turn the back of the left hand downward to shut the clubface even more. This unorthodox action will reduce the effective loft of the club and help you hit a hot stinger that splits the fairway and rolls a long way too.

Par-3
Tee Shots

Hitting a tee-shot into birdie position on long and short par-3 holes demands that you factor in the pin's position and location of any hazards bordering the green, think strategically, pick the right club, and play the right type of shot.

Short holes, designed so the player can hit the green on his first shot, then two-putt for par or one-putt for birdie, are called par-3s.

Par-3 holes usually feature bunkers to the sides of the green. However, sometimes there is either another bunker located behind the putting surface or a water hazard guarding the front of the green. Frequently, too, you'll find the greens on short holes much more undulating than

Japanese player Shigeki Maruyama, one of golf's best iron players, playing a challenging par-3 hole.

those on the other holes, making the tee shot even more challenging. The reasons:

1. If the hole is cut on the lower level of a big two-tier green, and your tee-shot finishes on the top portion of the putting surface, you'll face a difficult two-putt situation.

2. Should your tee-shot finish on the lower level of the green, and the hole is on the top back plateau, you'll also have to hit an excellent lag putt to prevent three-putting and scoring a bogie.

Side slopes play a major role, too, on short holes. The experienced golfer knows that a medium length or short uphill putt is easier to play than a downhill putt. Consequently, he or she hits a controlled tee shot that either lands short of the cup and stops below the hole, or lands beyond the cup then spins back past the hole so that a more aggressive uphill putt can be hit. Furthermore, when a bunker or hazard is on the same side of the green as the hole, the good golfer knows it's best to work the ball from the "open" side of the green back toward the hole. That way, should the soft fade or soft draw not come off as planned, the player is still left with a relatively simple chip to set up a par putt.

Let's now work on building up your shot-making arsenal, so that you are prepared to handle any par-3 situation.

○ *SHOT 9: ONE-IRON LASER*

Situation: You face a 200-yard tee-shot to a firm, fast-running green featuring bunkers left and right. There is a clear entrance-way in the front of the green and the pin is on the lower level.

Strategy: The 1-iron is the perfect club to hit, since its lower loft will allow the ball to land just short of the green, then bounce a couple times before rolling to the hole.

Here are the swing secrets three-time U.S. Open winner Hale Irwin showed me for playing this shot, when I, as senior instruction editor at *GOLF Magazine*, worked on an article with him.

Shot-Technique Tip: Irwin told me that you must:

1. Keep the club moving low to the ground in the takeaway, for about twelve inches, to program power into the swing, via the creation of a wide arc.

2. Employ a full on-balanced backswing action, making sure to keep the left wrist flat so the clubface stands a better chance of finishing square to the target.

3. Keep your head behind the ball through impact to ensure a solid upswing hit.

○ SHOT 10: THREE-METAL ROCKET

Situation: You face a tee-shot on a long par-3 that requires you to hit the ball 200 yards in the air to carry a water hazard in front of the green. The problem is you usually hit fairway clubs on a low trajectory.

Strategy: Visualize yourself hitting an extra-high and powerful rocket shot.

Shot-Technique Tip: Take a page out of Michelle Wie's lesson book and make this change to your grip. Slide your right forefinger down and under the grip so that it's separated from your middle finger.

Swing back normally.

On the downswing, you'll be surprised how this new grip alteration increases your power and adds height to your shot.

SHOT 11: LEFT-TO-RIGHT CROSSWIND CONTROL-PLAY

Situation: You face a mid-iron shot into a 20-mph, left-to-right crosswind.

Strategy: To cheat the wind and hit the ball close to the cup, you must play a sharp turning draw into the wall of wind blowing from the left, by following the example set by former British Open champion David Duval.

Shot-Technique Tip: Set up closed, aiming your body and club twenty yards right of the green. Swing the club back on a very flat path and plane and stop when reaching the three-quarter position.

Swing out at the ball. In the hitting area, rotate your right hand and forearm vigorously in a counterclockwise direction so that you close the clubface at impact and impart controlled draw-spin on the ball.

25

Michelle Wie (pictured) illustrates how a trigger finger grip, also used by high-ball power hitter John Daly, promotes a strong body-club release through impact.

GOLFWEEK'S 101 WINNING GOLF TIPS

PAR-3 TEE SHOTS

SHOT 12: RIGHT-TO-LEFT CROSSWIND CONTROL-PLAY

Situation: You face a mid-iron shot into a 20-mph, right-to-left crosswind.

Strategy: To cheat the wind and hit the ball close to the cup, you must play a sharp turning fade into the wall of wind blowing from the right, by following these simple instructions given to me by golfing great Ken Venturi.

Shot-Technique Tip: Set up open, with your body and the club aimed twenty yards left of target.

Make a compact, upright backswing.

Swing down across the ball, with your left elbow winged out and the back of your left hand bowed outward to help you hold the clubface open and hit a controlled fade into the crosswind.

SHOT 13: MID-IRON BACK-UP

Situation: The hole on a 160-yard par-3 is cut only fifteen feet behind a water hazard fronting the lower front portion of the green.

Strategy: Focus on a landing area behind the hole. Your objective is to hit that "bull's eye," so that you guarantee avoiding the water and, more importantly, spin the ball back to the hole.

28

One golfer who can really spin the ball is Chad Campbell. Therefore, follow these instructions, based on what I concluded are this young superstar's setup and swing secrets after observing him in action.

Shot-Technique Tip: At address, select the club you hit 170 yards with and tee the ball low.

Swing the club back on an exaggerated upright angle, allowing your wrists to hinge freely as you employ a compact action.

At the start of the downswing, increase the pressure in your left-hand grip and then pull the club down into the back of the ball. This type of swing allows you to make solid contact at impact, take a divot after impact, and impart exaggerated backspin on the ball.

○ SHOT 14: MID-IRON "RELEASER"

Situation: You face a 170-yard shot to an undulated two-tier green. The hole is on the top level of the putting surface and there's no hazard guarding its front entranceway.

Strategy: Here, rather than attacking the flag and running the risk of overshooting the hole, do what I've observed golf's number-one woman player, Annika Sorenstam, do in this situation: Hit a shot that lands short and then bounces three times before releasing to the hole.

29

Shot-Technique Tip: Set your feet and body slightly closed to the target.

Swing the club back to the inside, stopping at the three-quarter point to enhance control.

Trigger the downswing by clearing your left hip vigorously. Also, be sure to freely release your right hand and right arm so that you close the clubface in the impact zone and impart a slight degree of over-spin on the ball.

○ SHOT 15: HIT-TO-HELL TEE BALL

Situation: You're standing on an elevated tee of a fairly short par-3 hole, looking down at a green that's at sea level.

Strategy: The execution of this shot requires that you take less club than normal for the designated distance appearing on the scorecard. The bigger the drop in elevation, the weaker the club you should play. Why? The steep drop reduces the effective length of the hole.

Shot Technique Tip: Tee the ball lower and make a shorter, smoother swing than normal, just like Japanese tour golfer Shigeki Maruyama does when playing an iron shot from an elevated tee on a par-3 hole.

○ SHOT 16: HIT-TO-HEAVEN TEE BALL

30

Situation: You're standing on a tee looking up at a green 140 yards away and twenty yards above sea level.

Choosing less club and swinging rhythmically allows Fred Funk to hit good shots on challenging par-3 holes, like the one he's playing here.

Strategy: The execution of this shot requires that you take two clubs more (i.e., a 6-iron rather than 8-iron) to make up for the lay of the land's sharp incline, increasing the effective length of the hole.

Shot-Technique Tip: Tee the ball higher and employ a longer, more upbeat swing, just like South African–born star Ernie Els does when competing at venues around the world.

3

Fairway
Plays

Different types of fairway grasses, ever changing lies, various angles of approaches onto greens, long and short distances to the hole, the position of the flagstick, the condition of the green, and slopes in the putting surface all determine your choice of shot.

Regardless of how precise you hit drives on par-4 holes, shooting low scores depends greatly on hitting fairway shots the correct distance and on the correct line.

Many club-level golfers are under the impression that hitting a good fairway shot is simply a matter of figuring out the distance to the hole, choosing a club that allows you to hit the ball the required distance, and employing your normal swing. Wrong!

Michelle Wie in the Fairway.

Because golf courses feature slopes in the fairway, trees at the corner of the dogleg that may require you to hit a low shot or high shot to avoid hitting its branches, a more severe hazard to one side of a green, or wind to deal with, each and every shot—long or short—requires that you think clearly and creatively. So yes, of course you need to choose the right club. But more importantly, you need to employ the specific type of setup and swing that's required for hitting a particular ideal shot.

Top tour professionals realize that the correct fairway-play strategy means you must sometimes choose a stronger or weaker club than normal, open or close the clubface at address, swing the club on a flat or upright plane, or accelerate your hands and arms faster or slower through impact. In short, to be a good fairway-player, you must learn to adapt to the lie and be able to improvise.

Aside from being imaginative and highly skilled, one common thread between great fairway shot-makers past and present is knowing precisely how far they hit the ball with each club; when they open the clubface, choke down on the handle, grip lightly, grip firmly, swing fast or swing slow, make a half swing, three-quarter length action, or full swing.

The only way you can raise your own game to such a sophisticated level, and become a master at playing long and short fairway shots, is to sacrifice some playing time for practice time. Pay closest attention to learning the art of improvisation, so you know just what combination of club, setup, and swing produce each type of shot. Take things in stride, learning something new each session until you finally program so much good data into your brain that you are fully prepared for any fairway lie you that confronts you on the course.

Another asset great fairway shot-makers share is a one-shot-at-a-time philosophy. Tiger Woods plays so much in the "now" that he is oblivious to distractions, just as Jack

Nicklaus was during his heyday and Severiano Ballesteros, too, whom many golf aficionados consider the
greatest shot-maker of all time.

I played a round of golf with Seve in 1986, at Spain's
LaManga Golf Club, when he was in top form. I can as-
sure you that when Seve played fairway specialty shots he
was all business. I could see by the look in his eyes as he
analyzed the situation that he was grinding away mentally.
Then, to my astonishment, he closed his eyes while making practice swings, telling me he was putting himself into
some kind of trance. Once he opened his eyes again, star-
ing at the ball then the target as he prepared to swing, you
could see he was in his own little world. It was really
something to watch. In fact, as he told me after the round,
on that day, like in tournaments, he concentrated so hard
that he entered a cocoon or "bubble."

"Ever since boyhood, when often I felt as if I lived in a
cocoon-like state inside some kind of bubble, concentration has been a strong part of my game," said Seve.

"Nowadays, by the time a tournament arrives, I'm so
deeply immersed in my game plan and my play that I'm
virtually oblivious to outside sights and sounds.

"The first time since childhood I was able to envelop myself in the cocoon was during the 1979 British Open at Royal
Lytham & St. Annes—a championship I won thanks to iso-
lated concentration that enabled me to hit fairway shots at
will, land the ball close to the hole, and convert birdie putts."

Another plus-factor common to exceptionally good fairway shot-makers, is a sense of touch or feel, often developed by practicing from a young age with one club, such as a 5-iron. This experimental trial-and-error process of self-teaching enabled Ballesteros, and will enable you, to discover a number of swing keys that can be applied to all types of fairway shots; everything from the Driver-off-the-Deck Long Approach to the Pitching Wedge Curve-Right Ball, both of which I will address in this chapter.

In order to evolve into a true fairway shot-making virtuoso, you must be bold enough to add your own personal nuances to your technique. For example, the young Spanish superstar Sergio Garcia "milks" the club by gripping and re-gripping it a couple of times to enhance his feel. Tiger Woods employs a couple of miniature swings before setting up, to relax and get in the right rhythm. Phil Mickelson analyzes the lie and the shot-making situation intently, to help him make the right mental calculations relative to the distance of the shot and the type of club and swing needed to hit the ball precisely at the target.

Exactly what personal nuance you add to your routine does not matter. What does matter is that by the time you are ready to set up to play a fairway shot, you are sure you have the right club in your hands and are ready to make the swing you know will work best, based on the good feeling it gave you when you rehearsed it prior to addressing the ball.

Now that you understand that there really is no one simple formula that always applies when hitting fairway shots into greens, let me begin today's lesson and teach you a variety of shots that sooner or later you will need to play in order to beat the course and shoot the scores you previously only dreamed about.

○ *SHOT 17: DRIVER-OFF-THE-DECK LONG APPROACH*

Situation: You face a long approach to a par-4 hole; so long, in fact, that you know you will not reach the green with your trusty number-3 fairway metal club.

Strategy: Here, be aggressive and play a driver off the fairway grass, by following these instructions given to me by two time British Open champion Greg Norman.

Shot-Technique Tip: Play the ball opposite your left in-step, rather than off your left heel. This small adjustment will encourage a low takeaway, thereby allowing you to create the desired wide arc of swing. Playing the ball up will also allow you to hit the ball more powerfully on the upswing.

Any swing changes? Yes. Grip the club very light to promote an extra-free, extra-fluid release. Otherwise, swing the driver as you would normally.

○ *SHOT 18: DOWN-UNDER FAIRWAY-METAL-PLAY*

Situation: The ball is 220 yards from the green, lying on tightly mowed fairway grass. You are hitting to a hole located on the top flat plateau of a severe undulated green with trouble surrounding the putting surface.

Strategy: You must hit the ball on a much higher trajectory than you would normally with a fairway metal club, in order to land the ball close to the hole and hold the green. Here's what I learned about playing this shot from golf legend Gary Player.

Shot-Technique Tip: Grip the club firmly with the pressure in your fingers about 7 on a 1–10 scale. Play the ball back about two inches behind your left heel with sixty percent of your body weight balanced on your left foot.

Swing the club back on a very upright angle, stopping when reaching the three-quarter point.

On the downswing, concentrate on leading the club into impact with your hands and coming into the ball sharply. Many amateur golfers try and hit fairway metal shots on the upswing and try to scoop the ball into the air. Gary showed me that by going down after the ball it's easy to pop it into the air. This shot-making wizard also convinced me that this shot allows you to be aggressive in a pressure situation and stop the ball quickly on the green.

39

40

Gary Player, truly a golf legend in his own time, executing the down-under fair-
way-metal shot.

SHOT 19: IRON "HIGH BALL"

Situation: The ball is sitting on fairway grass and you need to hit a high shot so that the ball carries a big bunker fronting the green.

Strategy: In this course situation, first visualize yourself hitting a high shot and follow these tips based on technical notes I made while observing the iron-swing of PGA Tour star and former U.S. Open champion Jim Furyk.

Shot-Technique Tip: At address, play the ball off your left instep. Also, set your hands and head behind the ball.

Extend the club back for a longer period of time in the takeaway and employ a three-quarter length backswing.

On the downswing, keep your head and upper body weight back while driving your legs toward the target. The tilt-action that results will allow you to stay behind the ball in the impact zone, drive your hands and club into a high finish, and propel the ball high into the air.

SHOT 20: LONG IRON "RUNNER"

Situation: You face a 4-iron shot on a par-5 hole and you know if you can get the ball running once it lands you can get home in two.

Strategy: Go for the green. You can hit the running shot if you follow these directions, based on what I learned

41

42

43

PGA Tour player Jim Furyk shows what impact and through-impact positions are required for hitting a powerfully accurate "high ball" iron shot.

from playing golf in Virginia with two-time U.S. Open champion Curtis Strange.

Shot-Technique Tip: To put some "heat" on the ball, take your normal long-iron setup and employ your normal full backswing.

On the downswing, exaggerate the releasing action of your right hand, right arm, and right forearm. That way, the toe of the club will lead its heel through impact and you will impart hot right-to-left sidespin on the ball.

○ *SHOT 21: BALL-ABOVE-FEET SIDEHIILL RECOVERY-PLAY*

Situation: The ball is on fairway grass, above the player's feet.

Strategy: Off this kind of lie, the tendency is for the ball to move from right to left. So take precautions at address by aiming the clubface and your body a few yards right of target.

Shot-Technique Tip: Choke down on the club for control, and set your weight more towards your toes to help you retain balance.

The lie itself will make your swing flatter, but it will not hurt to imagine yourself employing a more rounded action as you set up to the ball.

44

The swing should be governed almost entirely by your hands and arms, so keep your knees flexed and head down through impact. These vital keys, which I learned by observing tour pro Stuart Appleby swinging, will help you stay anchored and balanced.

The chief lesson to learn from looking at Shigeki Maruyama hit this side-hill lie shot is to stay down in the hitting area.

SHOT 22: BALL-BELOW FEET SIDEHILL RECOVERY-PLAY

Situation: The ball lies on fairway grass, below the player's feet.

Strategy: Off this kind of lie, the tendency is for the ball to fly from left to right, so allow for this type of curve by aiming your body and the clubface a few yards left of target.

Shot-Technique Tip: Stand closer to the ball (which should be positioned in the middle of your stance) to feel more in control of the swing and promote a more upright swing plane.

To preserve your balance, bend more at the knees, set your weight on your heels, and make a compact backswing.

In the downswing, it's vital to retain your exaggerated knee flex and keep your head still as you pull the club into the back of the ball.

SHOT 23: UPHILL IRON APPROACH

Situation: The ball sits on an uphill fairway lie, 190 yards from the hole.

Strategy: Choose one club more for the required distance (i.e., a 3-iron instead of 4-iron) to allow for the effective loft of the club being increased at impact.

46

Shot-Technique Tip: Play the ball off your higher foot, employ a full backswing, and swing up the slope, as per the instructions taught to me by John Anselmo, who was Tiger Woods' coach for many years.

SHOT 24: DOWNHILL IRON APPROACH

Situation: The ball sits on a downhill slope in the fairway, 190 yards from the hole.

Strategy: Choose one club less for the required distance (i.e., a 5-iron rather than a 4-iron) to allow for the effective loft of the club being decreased at impact.

Shot-Technique Tip: Play the ball opposite your higher foot, employ a super-controlled compact backswing, and swing down the slope, as per the instructions once given to me by legendary pro golfer Ray Floyd.

SHOT 25: WET-TURF "TAMER"

Situation: The ball is sitting on wet fairway grass, but not in enough moisture for you to declare the ball to be in casual water and get a free drop to a dry area. You are mid-iron range from the hole and you fear driving the clubhead into the soft turf and hitting a heavy shot.

Strategy: Visualize yourself sweeping the ball off the wet turf rather than digging down into the turf.

47

Shot-Technique Tip: Here, you need to take precautions against hitting a "fat" shot by setting your feet down in a closed position and playing the ball off your left instep rather than left heel.

On the backswing, simply turn your arms and shoulder on a flatter plane. By employing what top teacher Jim Hardy calls a one-plane swing, you will automatically come into impact on a shallow, more streamlined angle, and cleanly brush the ball off the grass.

◯ *SHOT 26: SHORT-IRON "ZIPPER" SHOT*

Situation: You are 7-iron distance from the hole, and you face a shot over a deep bunker fronting the green. The hole is on the lower level of the green.

Strategy: Here, *carry* and *spin* are your buzz words. In short, you must hit the ball beyond the hole, and spin it back a full twenty feet.

Shot-Technique Tip: Hold the club, using a weak grip. Play the ball back in your stance, as much as midway between your feet, which should be spread less than normal.

Swing the club back on an exaggerated steep plane or angle.

Tailoring the Tip: Former British Open champion David Duval, who I'm happy to see is on the come-back trail, is a master at playing the Zipper Shot. LPGA player Morgan Pressel is also darn good at hitting this shot.

48

Swing the club down on the same steep plane, but be sure to pull hard with your hands that, for best results, should be leading the club into the ball.

○ *SHOT 27: PITCHING WEDGE "SLIDER"*

Situation: The ball is in the middle of the fairway, sitting on closely-shaven grass and 100 yards from the flagstick. The hole is located on the back top corner of a two-tier green.

Strategy: This shot calls for you to be aggressively cautious. You want to shoot at the flag, yet take something off the shot to avoid a hot "shooter" that could fly as far as twenty yards over the green.

Shot-Technique Tip: Set up open to the target line. Put 70 percent of your weight on your left foot and position your hands several inches ahead of the clubhead to encourage an upright backswing and sharp angle of descent. Aim the clubface at the hole, but set it down slightly open.

Swing the club back away from your body, stopping at the three-quarter point.

Swing your arms, hands, and club down from outside-to-inside, so that you impart left to right sidespin on the ball and it slides toward the hole.

49

Scott Hoch, one of golf's best iron-shot control players on the PGA Tour, plays the Slider fantastically.

○ SHOT 28: SAND WEDGE CURVE-LEFT BALL

Situation: The ball is sitting up in the fairway seventy-five yards from the hole. The pin is in the left-hand corner of a green, behind a deep bunker.

Strategy: Instead of playing safe and hitting to the "fat" of the green, right of the flag, set up a birdie opportunity by getting the ball to curve left in the air, bounce, and roll toward the hole, as shot-making maestro Chi Chi Rodriguez taught me how to do when we played together in Naples, Florida.

Shot-Technique Tip: Aim your body at an area of green several yards right of the hole. Aim the clubface at the flag, but close it slightly. Swing normally. Watch the ball turn toward "birdie land."

○ SHOT 29: PITCHING WEDGE CURVE-RIGHT BALL

Situation: Your ball is sitting up in the fairway, 100 yards from the green. The pin is on the right hand corner of a green, tucked behind a deep bunker.

Strategy: Instead of hitting to the "fat" of the green, set up a birdie opportunity by getting the ball to turn right in the air, bounce, and roll toward the hole.

Shot-Technique: Aim your body at the fat of the green. Aim your clubface at the flag, but open it up slightly.

Swing normally and watch the ball turn toward "birdie-land."

Incidentally, I also learned this shot from Chi Chi!

Trouble-Play Techniques

Even the game's top golf professionals miss fairways and greens, so like Tiger Woods and his fellow PGA Tour players, you'd better be prepared for any course situation by learning how to hit long, medium, and short shots from what veteran ABC golf commentator Peter Alliss calls "spots of bother."

In my heart, I know that I'd like to play one perfect round. Even the great Ben Hogan dreamed of scoring birdie on all eighteen holes. In my head, however, I know that neither the game of golf nor the golf swing was designed for total perfection. I guess then that watching golfers like me and you deal with the challenge of recovering from trouble is what keeps the golfing gods laughing.

Severiano Ballesteros, golf's all-time greatest on-course escape artist, doing what he does best.

All it takes is a bad swing or a bad bounce on a drive or an approach to miss the fairway or green and find your ball in trees, rough, water, sand, or some other trouble spot.

No matter how technically sound and grooved your swing, during a round of golf you are bound to miss some fairways and greens. At such times that the timing or rhythm of your swing lets you down, or you make another type of mistake that causes the ball to finish in trouble, you will be required to dig deep mentally in order to keep a cool head and play the smartest long or short recovery shot from what the pros call the "junk."

The fact is, often the golfer finds the ball in trouble because of failing to plan out a shot sensibly in advance. For example, on a sharp dogleg-left hole, the golfer hits the drive through the fairway into trouble only because he or she should have teed off with a number-3 fairway metal club or opted to hit a draw shot with a driver around the corner of the dogleg, instead of trying to boom the ball far down the center of the winding fairway, especially a narrow one.

In addressing the subject of approach shot mistakes, the most common error I witness over and over occurs when the player finds the ball sitting down in light rough, mid-iron distance from the green. Typically, the player chooses to aggressively attack a hole tucked in the right corner of the green instead of choosing the fat area of green left of

55

the flag as the target and not flirting with the trouble near the hole-side of the putting surface.

Some club-level players also fall victim to their egos when hitting a second shot into a short par-4 hole or third shot into a par-5. The classic mistake is to watch a golfer try to hit a wedge as hard as is physically possible, instead of swinging a 9-iron smoothly or choking down on an 8-iron and then employing their normal swing. What happens? The player loses his or her balance, power is drained from the swing, and the ball often falls short of the green, landing in a sand bunker or water hazard.

Any good golfer knows that gambling on the golf course by hitting low percentage shots off the tee or into the green is a silly strategy that will inevitably lead to lost strokes and prevent you from lowering your handicap.

The top-notch tour golfer or low handicap player has learned through hard experience that being totally unrealistic and trying to hit the miracle shot is a sure sign of golfing immaturity and only compounds errors. Still, these same golfers, again through experience, have learned to differentiate between what former golfing great Johnny Miller calls "red light" situations that signal a golfer to play safe and "green light" situations that signal a go-for-it strategy.

Sheer common sense, if not experience, should make you realize that course situations can only be considered green light situations if the lie of the ball tells you that you

56

have a good chance of hitting a good recovery shot, or that your confidence level is high because you have taken the time to do what most amateur golfers rarely ever do: practice hitting long and short trouble shots out of every conceivable bad lie.

Onlookers at golf tournaments are awestruck watching Tiger Woods pull off the impossible looking shot, just as they used to be when Seve Ballesteros did the same en route to winning three British Open and two Masters championships as well as numerous tournaments around the world. Folks, please understand that the reason these two great golfers became masterful trouble players is because they trained themselves to read lies, learned through trial-and-error which clubs work best in certain course situations, and practiced until playing trouble shots became as routine as hitting drives off a tee or approach shots from the center of a manicured fairway. You should do the same.

I'm not going to go on record as saying that practice makes perfect and that you can prepare yourself for any bad lie, because new ones do pop up from time to time. That's just the nature of the game of golf. Because fairways seem to be getting narrower and greens smaller these days, it's more likely that you are bound to find yourself in trouble a few times during a round.

What follows in this chapter is a guidebook for learning how to hit a wide variety of long- and short-range trouble shots, from awkward lies bordering the fairway to bad and ugly lies near the green. In presenting these shots, I've put down what I believe are the tools for you to work with for your entire golfing life. And, I do a lot more than simply teach you how to analyze a lie, pick the right club, and choose the right type of swing. In conducting my trouble play lessons, and sharing these tips with you, I also teach you the importance of mental imagery and understanding the causes and effects of specific setups and swings. That way, from here on in, when you face a difficult lie, you'll possess the secrets to being an on-course Houdini.

○ *SHOT 30: FAIRWAY-DEPRESSION RECOVERY PLAY*

Situation: The ball is in the middle of the fairway, 200 yards from the green, in a slight depression.

Strategy: When the ball lands in a grassy dip in the fairway grass, accept the fact that to hit the best recovery shot, you must change your swing and play a 3-metal fairway club rather than a long iron or 5-metal fairway club. Swinging the club on an inside-square-inside path, as you normally do on this length shot off fairway grass, will not work here. You must alter your swing path and follow these instructions which I developed through my own experimentation when practicing this shot.

> *Tailoring the Tip:* The technique described above will allow you to hit a solid golf shot. However, the ball will fade to the right, so allow for this when setting up and aiming the clubface.

58

Shot-Technique Tip: Set up open to the target line, with your feet, knees, hips, and shoulders pointing left of target.

Swing the club back outside the target line.

Swing down across the target line to avoid the protruding area of ground behind the ball.

◯ *SHOT 31: HYBRID-HIT*

Situation: The ball is in light rough, 190 yards from the green.

Strategy: Rather than play a wedge and hit the ball safely to the fairway, play your 7-metal hybrid club and go for the green! This club is designed with a heavier sole, so it will allow you to lift the ball out of light rough more easily, as top LPGA players prove every week when competing on tour.

Shot-Technique Tip: Play the ball midway between your feet, with your hands out ahead of it and 70 percent of your weight on your left foot.

To help you swing the club back on the upright plane that's needed for this shot, tilt your left shoulder downward as you turn your body on the backswing.

In swinging down, simultaneously pull the club down into the slot and drop your right shoulder dramatically. Because you'll hit the ball cleanly on the descent, it will pop out of the rough and fly fast off the clubface.

SHOT 32: FAIRWAY BUNKER-PLAY SWEEP

Situation: The ball is sitting up in a fairway bunker featuring a low lip, 180 yards from the hole.

Strategy: Here, due to the low lip, you can and should hit a 5-fairway metal club and go for the green, provided you learn and groove the following technique.

Shot-Technique Tip: Set up slightly closed with the ball positioned opposite your left heel.

On the backswing, make a low takeaway, then swing the club back to the top on a shallow path.

On the downswing, rotate your left hip counterclockwise to open up a clear passageway for you to swing the club back into the ball on a shallow arc and sweep it cleanly off the sand.

SHOT 33: CLOVER-RECOVERY-PLAY

Situation: The ball sits in a light clover patch 175 yards from the green.

Strategy: To compensate for leaves of clover interfering with the ball and clubface at impact and causing a flyer shot, choose a more lofted club than normal (e.g., a 6-iron instead of a 5-iron).

Shot-Technique Tip: You want to mitigate the flyer-factor, so go with a flatter rather than steeper swing. To help you promote this type action, simply think of rotating your shoulders in a clockwise direction on the backswing and a counterclockwise direction on the downswing, as renowned golf instructor Phil Ritson taught me.

◯ SHOT 34: THE "CHASER"

Situation: The ball lies on a patch of threadbare sandy rough, approximately 170 yards from the green.

Strategy: The tendency is to swing the club on a steep angle and try to dig the ball out. That's the wrong approach. You want to, ultimately, chase the ball with the club in the hitting area.

Shot-Technique Tip: In recovering from this lie, set up slightly closed, swing the club back on a flat path, and swing through the ball, keeping the club low to the ground.

Spanish superstar and two time Masters champion Jose Maria Olazabal plays this shot superbly; I think because he's a natural "sweeper" of the ball.

◯ SHOT 35: OUT-OF-DIVOT RECOVERY

Situation: The ball is in a fairway divot, 150 yards from the green.

Strategy: To hit down extra-sharply into the back of the ball with the clubface's sweet spot, just as Tiger Woods does when facing this lie.

61

Shot-Technique Tip: In setting up, play the ball in the middle of a narrow stance and lean your weight into your left leg.

Make a compact, upright backswing action, letting your wrists be lively and your left heel lift off the ground slightly.

Start the downswing by re-planting your left heel. This trigger will promote a strong leverage action and promote accelerated arm-action that, in turn, will allow you to bring the club sharply into the back of the ball.

○ *SHOT 36: FAIRWAY BUNKER MID-IRON HIT*

Situation: The ball sits in a fairway bunker featuring a fairly high lip, 160 yards from the green.

Strategy: Think: "Hit the ball before the sand." This swing key and the others that follow were taught to me by former Masters winner Craig Stadler, best known as "The Walrus" of the Champions Tour.

Tailoring the Tip: Mark O'Meara, former winner of the Masters and British Open, is one of the best of all PGA Tour pros at playing this shot.

Shot-Technique Tip: Take a stronger club than normal, open your stance, and open the clubface slightly.

Swing the club back with your arms, on a very steep plane angle.

Tiger Woods, employing a sharp descending blow of club-to-ball, to recover from a divot.

TROUBLE-PLAY TECHNIQUES

On the downswing, minimize you lower body action and maximize your arm-swing.

Keep your head behind the ball, as you squeeze the grip more firmly with your left hand and pull the club down into the back of the ball.

○ *SHOT 37: WEDGE BLAST*

Situation: You face an approach shot of 155 yards, from rough. The ball is so far down in the grass that even a lofted utility club will not help you recover.

Strategy: You must play a wedge and use a special technique favored by top tour professionals.

Shot-Technique Tip: The chief address key is to set your left or forward hip well open to the target line; this small alteration will open up a clear passageway for you to deliver the club freely and aggressively into the impact zone.

The chief backswing keys are letting your right wrist hinge to the max and allowing your left arm to bend.

The chief downswing keys are re-hinging both the right wrist and left elbow, as these moves will add snap to your swing and allow you to chop the ball out of the deep grass.

Golfers who naturally swing the club on an upright plane, such as professionals Nick Price and Adam Scott, play this shot exceptionally well.

64

SHOT 38: HEATHER-HIT

Situation: The ball lies in heather, mid-iron distance from the green.

Strategy: Take an 8-iron and accept the fact that hitting a solid lay-up shot in front of the green will still allow you to salvage par. Former British Open and Masters champion Sandy Lyle gave me this advice, as well as these instructions for playing this type of shot.

Shot-Technique Tip: Open the clubface to compensate for the heather grabbing the neck of the club and twisting it closed at impact.

On the backswing, encourage a strong turn by rotating your left shoulder past the ball.

On the downswing, drive your legs toward the target and let your hands lead the club into the ball. Also, hold on more firmly with both hands to prevent the clubface from really shutting down.

SHOT 39: BENTGRASS REVOVERY # 1

Situation: The ball is in bentgrass rough, common to courses in the northeast, lying 9-iron distance to the hole. The grass is growing toward the target.

Strategy: While most amateurs choose to play a more lofted club here, they shouldn't. Instead, I recommend that you stick with the 9-iron but accept the fact that you are going to take something off the shot by changing your swing slightly.

Shot-Technique Tip: Swing the club on an out-to-in path, rather than your normal inside-square-inside path, so that you hit a slight fade.

This technique will promote a high, soft-landing shot.

Being from the northeast, where bent grass is the norm, I taught myself this shot and the one that follows.

○ *SHOT 40: BENTGRASS RECOVERY # 2*

Situation: The ball is in long bentgrass rough, lying 9-iron distance to the hole. However, this time, the grass is growing toward you.

Strategy: Here, you must accept that the grass will reduce your clubhead speed and also cause the clubhead to twist shut at impact.

So, select two clubs less; in this case, a 7-iron.

Shot-Technique Tip: At address, play the ball just beyond the midpoint in your stance, so that your hands are a full three inches ahead of the ball.

Swing the club up to the three-quarter point on a very steep plane. Let your right elbow "fly" away from your body to increase your turn and build more torque and power into your action.

On the downswing, concentrate on keeping your upper left arm tight to your chest as you pull the club into the ball as fast as possible while maintaining good balance.

○ *SHOT 41: LOW BALL ESCAPE*

Situation: The ball is in semi-rough, 135 yards from the green, and overhanging tree limbs block your line to the green. You're playing the final hole of a match-play event and tied with your opponent whose ball lies in the middle of the fairway.

Strategy: The match is on the line, so be aggressive and go for the green by hitting an extra-low shot, rather than just pitching back to the fairway.

One thing: Don't swing until you see, in your mind's eye, the ball flying under the branches all the way to the green. Former PGA Tour player Gary Hallberg taught me this key, as well as the following secrets to success.

Shot-Technique Tip: At address, hood the clubface of a 4-iron to ensure a low trajectory and plenty of roll.

Keep your lower body almost perfectly still and wrist action to a minimum on the backswing. Stop swinging when your hands reach chest height.

Swing the club down and drive the clubhead low to the ground through impact.

○ *SHOT 42: PINE-NEEDLE SURVIVOR SHOT*

Situation: You are 125 yards from the green, but the ball lies on loosely-knitted pine needles.

Strategy: Be smart and keep the club above the needles at address, to prevent the ball from moving and causing you to be penalized. Also, concentrate on the back center portion of the ball, because you must hit the ball cleanly, as John Gerring, one of golf's top teachers taught me when he was based at the Atlanta Country Club.

Shot-Technique Tip: Swing the club sharply upward, allowing your right wrist to hinge early in the takeaway.

Swing the club down quite aggressively with your hands and arms. Be sure not to make a strong weight shift or depend on foot action too much, or else you could slide out of position and miss-hit the shot.

○ *SHOT 43: SHORT IRON KNOCKDOWN*

Situation: You are 120 yards away from the green with just enough breeze in you face, say 10 mph, to wreak havoc with your shot-making game plan.

Strategy: Here, you want to hit the ball under the wind, but by making only small setup and swing adjustments. And, if you heed the following instructions given to me by former CBS golf analyst Ken Venturi, you can play the same club you would normally hit from 120 yards.

68

Shot-Technique Tip: In setting up, play the ball in the middle of your stance, put 60 percent of weight on your left foot, and choke down on the club for maximum control.

Tailoring the Tip: Irish pro-golf stars Padraig Harrington and Darren Clarke play this shot wonderfully; I suppose owing to their experience playing links golf in windy conditions.

On the backswing, extend the club in the takeaway and employ a shallow compact swing.

On the downswing, drive your legs toward the target, being careful not to lunge forward, then lead the club into the ball with your hands.

○ *SHOT 44: BERMUDA GRASS BAIL-OUT*

Situation: The ball sits in Bermuda grass rough, ninety yards from the hole situated behind a bunker.

Strategy: This type of coarse rough demands that you play a pitching wedge because it features a sharp leading edge.

Shot-Technique Tip: Take your normal wedge-address position, but open the clubface to compensate for it closing at impact.

Swing the club back and down on a steeper plane and swing faster than normal to cut though the Brillo-type rough.

69

PGA Tour player Davis Love is very good at playing this shot.

○ *SHOT 45: "ROUNDHOUSE"*

Situation: The ball is under the branches of a bush, so that you are unable to take a normal stance.

Strategy: Don't take an unplayable lie penalty. You can hit a good shot from this lie if you follow these directions given to me by Severiano Ballesteros when we collaborated on the book *Natural Golf*:

Shot-Technique Tip: Take a 6-iron, kneel down with your arms outstretched and lock your hips to promote a fluid all-arms swing.

Swing the club back and through on a flat "roundhouse" type plane, keeping your wrists locked.

Swing down, again controlling the action totally with your arms and being sure to rotate your right shoulder under your chin through impact.

○ *SHOT 46: THE "RUNNER"*

Situation: The ball is perched up high on an uncut tuft of fairway grass, fifty yards from a hole cut on the lower level of a two-tier green.

Strategy: Play a 7-iron running shot, instead of playing a lofted club and risking hitting the ball too high and falling short of the green.

Shot-Technique Tip: Set up square to the ball and target. Play the ball back in a shoulder-width stance with your hands just slightly ahead of the clubhead.

Swing the club back low only a short distance while allowing your right wrist to hinge just slightly.

On the downswing, nudge your weight left, straighten the right wrist at impact, and most importantly, keep the club moving low through the hitting area, as Tiger Woods' former coach Butch Harmon taught me.

◯ *SHOT 47: HARDPAN HIT*

Situation: The ball is forty yards from the green and sitting on hardpan. You must carry a bunker and stop the ball quickly next to the hole.

Strategy: Play a lob wedge rather than a sand wedge because it features a sharper leading edge and additional loft.

Shot-Technique Tip: Set up open with the clubface open too.

Swing the club back along a narrow arc.

Hit down sharply on the ball, holding back the follow-through. This hit-and-hold action that I've observed PGA

Tour star Phil Mickelson depend on will allow you to nip the ball cleanly off hard ground.

○ SHOT 48: ROUGH RECOVERY

Situation: The ball is down in the rough, thirty-five yards from a pin cut behind a water hazard.

Strategy: Avoid trying to hit a miracle shot stiff to the hole. Your priority is to carry the water and land the ball somewhere on the green.

Shot-Technique Tip: With the ball positioned forward in the stance, align your body open. Also, open the face of a sand wedge to further program loft into the shot.

Swing the club back to the halfway position, keeping your left arm extended and allowing your right wrist to hinge immediately in the takeaway.

Pull the club down with both hands and drive your right shoulder under your chin. Ideally, you want the club to contact an area of grass about an inch behind the ball. Exaggerate the follow-through to help propel the ball upward.

I taught myself this shot, and after hitting lots of practice shots came to the conclusion that the sand wedge works better than the pitching wedge or lob wedge.

72

○ SHOT 49: ICE PLANT "CHOP"

Situation: The ball lies thirty yards from the green in ice plant, common on California golf courses such as Cypress Point.

Strategy: This lie is so deadly that George Peper, the former editor-in-chief of *Golf Magazine* once compared hitting out of ice plant to hitting a shot out of a pile of sneakers. Understandably, then, your mindset should be to extract the ball from the ice plant lie and back to the fairway on your first shot. Hitting the green is a bonus, and you have a chance to reach it if you heed the following directions to the letter.

Shot-Technique Tip: The best way to recover is to take a lob wedge, play the ball back in an very open and narrow stance, swing the club up on an exaggerated steep plane, and swing down as fast as you can using a chopping action. You should actually feel as if you are bringing down an axe to split a log.

○ SHOT 50: BARE LIE GREENSIDE RECOVERY

Situation: The ball lies on a bare spot, amidst nicely manicured fringe grass, only twenty-five feet from the hole.

Strategy: Select a lob wedge and follow these three steps taught to me by John Daly. If you do, the ball will

73

pop up softly into the air, land near the hole, and stop quickly.

Shot-Technique Tip:

Step 1: Play the ball back in an open stance, with your hands a full three inches ahead of the clubhead.

Step 2: Employ a compact backswing, letting your right wrist hinge immediately in the takeaway.

Step 3: Re-hinge your right wrist early in the downswing, since this will promote a sharp descending hit.

○ *SHOT 51: THE "PITCH-OUT"*

Situation: You face a twenty yard pitch out of rough and you must carry a ten-foot-high tree in front of you.

Strategy: Here, you need to get the ball up quickly, so before you even start your swing visualize the ball flying high and carrying the tree.

Shot-Technique Tip: At address, open the face of a sand wedge, take an open stance, play the ball off your front foot, position your head behind the ball, put 60 percent of your weight on your right foot, and set your hands slightly behind the ball.

Swing the club back outside the target line, up to the halfway position.

Accelerate your hands and arms on the way down and follow through fully.

74

○ SHOT 52: GRASSY SLOPE BLAST

Situation: The ball is buried in wispy grass on an uphill slope fifteen yards from the hole.

Strategy: Make up your mind that you must be aggressive on this shot and extremely positive, or else you will tense up and miss-hit the ball. That's what shot-making virtuoso Seve Ballesteros told me when we played golf together in Spain two decades ago.

Shot-Technique Tip: Position the ball off your left heel and set your body open to the target line.

The uphill lie will likely prevent you from planting your left foot firmly, so lean into the slope. Grip down on the shaft for control and close the clubface slightly to compensate for the clubface opening when it contacts the grass.

Swing the club back in one piece to knee-level, keeping your wrists firm and weight left.

Pull the club down and through with your hands and arms, making sure to direct the clubhead up the slope through impact. Yes, you have just played a "blast" out of grass much like you would from sand off the same type of uphill-lie.

○ SHOT 53: THE "LEFT-BANK" RECOVERY

Situation: You are stymied by a tree to the right of the green, so much so that you are prevented from taking a

One secret to hitting an accurate blast-shot from rough is to swing the club up the slope in the hitting area, as Seve Ballesteros does here.

normal setup and swing. The ball is to the side of the tree, so you can't even face it and hit a rebound shot. One option is to take an unplayable lie penalty and drop the ball, and hit three from the point of relief. Alternatively, you can hit the shot left-handed so that it flies low, hits the bank, and bounces up onto the green, and then you'd be left with a par putt.

Strategy: Assuming the state of the match is on the line and you must gamble, or you just want to try a fun shot, play this shot the southpaw way. Seve Ballesteros taught me how to play this shot when we collaborated on the book *Natural Golf*.

Shot-Technique Tip: Reverse your hand position on the grip end of a 7-iron, and turn the club over so its toe faces down and is in a position to hit the ball.

Once you set up, make essentially a long putting stroke action, using your arms to control the action and lively wrist action to promote feel. Two more things: let your hands lead the clubhead into the ball and keep your head down until after you hear the club contact the ball.

○ *SHOT 54: THE "SPLASH"*

Situation: You have just pulled the shot left of the green, into shallow water bordering its edge, and only half of the ball is above the surface. The ball is thirty-five feet from the hole.

Strategy: Since only half the ball is below the surface of the crater, you are in a green light course situation. Go!

Shot-Technique Tip: At address, set your feet narrowly apart with the ball back in your stance. Select a pitching wedge for this shot, since this club features less bounce than a sand wedge and a sharper leading edge that will more easily cut through the water. Hold the clubface open, but be sure to keep the clubhead above the water or else you will be penalized for grounding the ball in a hazard.

Make a short, steep-angled backswing.

Swing the club sharply down into a spot in the water only a half-inch behind the ball, so that you blast it out onto the green.

○ *SHOT 55: THE "REBOUNDER"*

Situation: The ball is so close to a tree trunk that you can't face the target and take your normal stance, making a normal swing and hitting directly at the green.

Strategy: Don't drop the ball and incur an unplayable lie penalty stroke. You can bounce the ball off the tree and bank it onto the green.

Shot-Technique Tip: To play the shot, face the tree trunk with your entire body aligned to the left of its trunk, so that you avoid getting hit with the ball after it rebounds. With a medium iron, make a slow, short, upright backswing, then swing the club down into the back of the ball using a "hit-and-hold" action of the hands at impact to stunt the follow-through.

○ SHOT 56: LONG BURIED LIE BUNKER SHOT

Situation: Half of the ball is submerged in the sand. The front bunker lip is relatively low and your ball is twenty-five yards from the hole.

Strategy: The buried lie calls for a digging action of the club into sand. Therefore, think: "Hit down sharply."

Shot-Technique Tip: Set up squarely to the ball with a pitching wedge, and align the clubface directly at your target. Just like when hitting out of shallow water, keep the club's head above the sand to avoid a penalty for grounding a club in a hazard. Play the ball back and set your hands well ahead of the club, with your weight left, to help promote a steep backswing.

Swing the club up and down on an extremely steep plane and pull the club down using your arms into a spot only a half-inch behind the ball. The ball will fly low and tend to run "hot," so you don't need to really pull hard on the club when swinging down.

No golfer I've ever played or worked with on instructional articles hits this shot and the two that follow better than Gary Player, whom many golf experts—and pros— rank as the best bunker player of all time.

79

SHOT 57: SHORT BURIED LIE BUNKER SHOT

Situation: Half of the ball is submerged in the sand. The front bunker lip is high and the ball is only twenty-five feet from the hole.

Strategy: Trust your swing, because you can hit the ball close to the hole from this lie.

Shot-Technique Tip: Set up square to the target line, with the ball opposite your left heel in a narrow stance. Position the ball in the middle of your stance with your hands slightly behind it. Turn the clubface in slightly, so its toe is ahead of its heel.

The key to the backswing is hinging the wrists early and swinging the sand wedge up on a very steep path and plane. (Relaxed grip pressure will help you accomplish these goals.)

Create acceleration by simultaneously rotating the hips in a counterclockwise direction and pulling down strongly with the left arm. As the clubhead penetrates the sand, it will open the clubface. This opening of the face very effectively works the club's flange underneath the ball, allowing you to miraculously impart stop-spin to it.

SHOT 58: UPHILL BUNKER-PLAY OUT

80

Situation: The ball sits up on a severe uphill slope forty feet from the green, and you fear catching the ball too cleanly and over-shooting the hole.

Spanish born Ryder Cup hero Sergio Garcia just might be the most talented player in the world when it comes to hitting a short bunker shot out of a buried lie, as he proves here.

Strategy: Don't let this lie get into your head.

Shot-Technique Tip: All this shot demands is that you play the ball opposite the instep of the higher foot, make a shallow backswing, hit a spot two inches behind the ball, and let the club follow the contour of the slope through the impact zone.

SHOT 59: DOWNHILL BUNKER-PLAY OUT

Situation: The ball sits on a severe downhill slope thirty feet from the hole, and you fear hitting down too sharply into the sand and leaving the ball in the bunker.

Strategy: Don't panic. You can hit this shot by following these simple instructions.

Shot-Technique Tip: All this shot demands is that you play the ball opposite the instep of your higher foot, employ an upright backswing, hit a spot in the sand four inches behind the ball, and swing down the slope through impact.

SHOT 60: THE "PEEK-A-BOO" SHOT

Situation: The ball is buried close to the front bunker wall.

Strategy: To land this ball anywhere on the green. Do not try to hit a finesse shot or you will pay the price.

Shot-Technique Tip: Play the ball well back in your stance and dig your feet down into the sand so you have a firm foundation to swing from. Lay the face of a sand wedge wide open, so it looks skyward. This will give you the loft needed to carry the ball out of the sand and over the lip.

Make a loose, three-quarter-length backswing by letting your wrists hinge.

Swing the club down as hard as you can into an area of sand a half-inch behind the ball. To help you stay behind the ball at impact use this mental image that 1965 British Open champion Henry Cotton made popular: try to peek under the ball as you swing the club down sharply into the sand.

SHOT 61: THE "KNIFE"

Situation: The ball is fully buried under the lip of a greenside bunker and there's fifteen feet of green between you and the hole.

Strategy: The sand wedge or even the pitching wedge will not work here because they feature bounce or added metal below the flange that prevents you from digging down deeply enough into the sand to hit a good recovery shot. The putter is the ideal club to hit what veteran golf pro Chi Chi Rodriguez calls a "knife shot." Here are the keys Chi Chi depends on when playing this wonderful shot.

Shot-Technique Tip: The key to the address is to point the toe of the putter at a spot in the sand directly behind the ball.

Swing the club straight up into the air on the backswing.

Pull the club straight down, so the toe of the putter's head strikes the sand directly behind the ball.

○ SHOT 62: ONE-FOOT-IN, ONE-FOOT-OUT BUNKER RECOVERY

Situation: The ball lies in the very back of the bunker, but in such an awkward position that you must keep one foot in and one foot out of the sand when playing this twenty-yard shot.

Strategy: You must think about staying down, maintaining good balance, and landing the ball somewhere on the green. It's no time to be overly aggressive.

Shot-Technique Tip: The most vital keys to the address are increasing the flex in your knees to stabilize the body, setting your right foot at a right angle to the target line to prevent the body from swaying to the right during the backswing, and gripping the club lightly to encourage good and lively hand action.

Once you feel sure that you are set up to the ball comfortably and correctly, with the ball positioned opposite the midpoint in your stance, make a compact backswing.

It's important to stay with the shot on the downswing, so maintain the flex in your knees and focus intently on your contact spot in the sand, about three inches behind the ball, as you swing fluidly through the impact zone.

PGA, LPGA, Champions Tour, and Nationwide Tour players make this shot look easy, simply because they practice hitting it. Follow their example.

○ *SHOT 63: HARD SAND HIT*

Situation: The ball lies in very hard sand, twenty feet from the hole.

Strategy: Forget depending on your normal bunker-play swing and using your sand wedge, and learn the following technique that will allow you to pinch the ball off this tricky lie and hit it close to the hole.

Shot-Technique Tip: Aim your body slightly left of target, position the ball closer to your right foot, set the clubface open, and put as much as 70 percent of your weight on your left foot when taking your address.

Swing the club back on a plane that is upright; more on the angle of a ferris wheel than a merry-go-round, to borrow an image from the famous British teacher John Jacobs.

Pull the club down hard into the back of the ball, holding on more tightly with your left hand to maintain a slightly open club position.

◯ *SHOT 64: SOFT SAND SHOT-SAVER*

Situation: The ball is in extra soft beach-type sand, thirty feet from the hole.

Strategy: Here, you must guard against digging down too deeply into the sand and, as a result, hitting a "fat" shot that stays in the bunker or finishes well short of the hole.

Shot-Technique Tip: Hold the club with a weak grip by turning your hands toward the target, so the Vs formed by your thumbs and forefingers point up at your chin. This one simple change will allow you to keep the clubface open in the hitting area so that you are able to slide it through the sand under the ball.

PGA Tour player Bob Tway, who holed a bunker shot on the final hole to win the 1986 PGA championship, is a good model for learning this shot.

◯ *SHOT 65: FRIED-EGG GREAT ESCAPE*

Situation: The ball sits in a crater of sand, almost like a yolk in the middle of an egg-white.

Strategy: Imagery is the key to success on this shot, as U.S. Open champion Ken Venturi taught me. If you heed the following advice he gave me, you will hit the ball out of the bunker with the greatest of ease and land it close to the hole.

Shot-Technique Tip: Imagine that there is the white of an egg around the ball. Next, use your normal bunker-play setup and backswing. Finally, and most importantly, swing the club into the white of the egg behind the ball then keep accelerating into a high finish so you take the yolk (ball) out with it.

◯ *SHOT 66: BUNKER PUTT*

Situation: The ball lies on packed, wet sand just twenty feet from the hole. The bunker's lip in front of you is low.

Strategy: Because the sand is wet, chipping is dangerous. In short, you could dig down too deeply and hit the shot fat. Putt the ball out, particularly since the bunker's lip is low.

Shot-Technique Tip: This greenside situation is best handled by making a slightly longer stroke than you would normally for the distance, and also swinging the putter on an exaggerated inside-inside path (favored by renowned putting coach Stan Utley), rather than a straight-back, straight-through path.

◯ *SHOT 67: LIFT-OFF*

Situation: The ball is sitting up in sand, but there is an extremely high lip in front of you and the hole is only fifteen feet from your ball.

Strategy: Trust this way of playing a unique shot that Seve Ballesteros taught me when we played together in Spain.

Shot-Technique Tip: Select a sand wedge. Choke down on the club's handle with your right hand gripping the club's shaft in a very strong position.

On the backswing, hinge your wrists early in the take-away so you swing the club on a steep angle.

On the downswing, un-hinge your right wrist early and turn your right hand under your left, to help you slide the club under the ball and lift it up quickly.

◯ *SHOT 68: 7-IRON SAND CHIP*

Situation: The ball lies on firm sand in a bunker with a low lip, only fifteen feet from the hole.

Strategy: Accept the fact that rather than playing a touch shot with a sand wedge, a chip with a 7-iron will work best.

Shot-Technique Tip: In playing this shot, pretend the ball is thirty feet from the hole to allow for the ball being slowed down somewhat by the lip; albeit one that is low.

Open your stance to give you a clearer picture of the line and promote a more free arms-controlled stroke.

Swing the club back low to the ground. Stop when the clubhead passes your right foot.

Swing the club down and through letting your hands play the lead role.

I learned how to hit this shot and the three that immediately follow by improvising during my practice sessions.

○ SHOT 69: LONG SANDY LIE CHIP

Situation: The ball is on a sandy area of fringe, owing to the grass being burnt out by the hot summer sun. You are ninety feet from the hole, with the ball sitting in an area that's level with the putting surface.

Strategy: Play a running chip with a 5- or 6-iron, depending on which gives you the most confidence and highest success rate.

Shot-Technique Tip: Set up square to the target. Hood the clubface, so the grooves are pointing more toward the ground than at the target.

Control the backswing and downswing totally with your arms, so that you let the loft of the club kind of hit the shot for you. You do not need to manipulate the club in any way with your hands.

○ SHOT 70: PART-SAND PART-GRASS RECOVERY

Situation: The ball lies in a mixture of sand and grass at the edge of a bunker only ten yards from the hole.

89

Strategy: In this situation, more than others, you must visualize the perfect shot playing out in your mind's eye, be super-confident that you can hit that shot, and totally commit to hitting it successfully. See yourself accelerating your arms on the downswing and hitting a high, soft-landing shot.

Shot-Technique Tip: Play the ball opposite your forward heel in an open stance, make a compact upright swing and, using just your arms, accelerate, the club into a spot only a half-inch behind the ball.

○ *SHOT 71: SAND CHIP "CHEATER"*

Situation: The ball lies in light rough, thirty feet from a hole cut out of a super-fast green, and there's a shallow low-lip bunker in your line.

Strategy: Here, run the ball through the sand with an 8-iron.

Shot-Technique Tip: Set up closed, with your body aligned right-of-target, and then aim the clubface straight at the hole.

Make a flat backswing.

In swinging down, turn your right hand and forearm counterclockwise to shut the clubface and impart a little hook-spin on the ball. You'll need to do that to make the ball scurry through the sand, bounce up onto the green, and roll to the hole.

Golf mega-star Phil "Lefty" Mickelson executing the part-sand part-grass recovery shot to perfection.

○ SHOT 72: "PICK"

Situation: The ball lies in a spot of threadbare fringe, twenty-five feet from the hole. You fear topping the ball, because there's no cushion underneath.

Strategy: You must pick the ball cleanly off the virtually bare fringe, rather than hit down on it with a sand wedge.

Shot-Technique Tip: Select a pitching wedge. Grip the club more firmly than normal. Play the ball two inches behind your left heel.

Swing the club back to waist height, keeping your body as still as is physically possible, controlling the motion almost entirely with your arms. Only let your right wrist hinge just slightly, as you will need to swing on a slight upright plane to be poised to bring the club down into the ball correctly.

Trigger the downswing by making a subtle shift of the hips toward the target. As you bring the club closer to the ball, let the right wrist straighten. Swing through fluidly, letting your arms take over, so that the pitching wedge lifts the ball into the air.

Tailoring the Tip: Golfers like former U.S. Open champion Michael Campbell of New Zealand, who swings the club on a flat plane, are normally better at hitting this shot than upright swingers.

◯ *SHOT 73: FAIRWAY METAL PUTT-CHIP*

Situation: The ball sits in the lush second cut of fringe grass only ten feet from the hole.

Strategy: Avoid hitting a shooter or flyer with a wedge or short iron. Depend instead on a lofted fairway metal club and rely on the following technique I've seen Vijay Singh and other top tour professionals employ when recovering.

Shot-Technique Tip: Set up the same way you would when hitting a short putt, only this time play the ball in the middle of your stance, and employ your usual stroke. The loft of the club will lift the ball over the heavier fringe and send it flying softly onto the green. From there it will roll to the hole like a putted ball.

○ SHOT 74: EQUATOR-HIT

Situation: The ball rests against the edge of the fringe grass bordering the green, fifteen feet from the hole.

Strategy: Here, selecting a pitching wedge and hitting a standard chip is not the smartest strategy. It's not time to choose a putter either. The reason these clubs will not work is that the fringe grass will hinder your backswing and prevent you from hitting a touch shot.

In this situation, you must play a sand wedge, taking advantage of its broader leading edge, and heed the following instructions I learned from former PGA Tour star Curtis Strange.

Shot-Technique Tip: Choke down on the club to promote added control and line its leading edge up with the ball's equator.

Swing the wedge straight back along the target line, keeping the clubhead low to the ground.

Swing the club through, using just your arms, so that you hit the top of the ball with the clubhead's flange.

93

○ SHOT 75: THE CONTROLLED TOP

Situation: The ball is sitting down in very coarse fringe and the hole is forty feet away.

Strategy: Here, you need to be creative and learn a shot taught to me by former British Open and Masters champion Sandy Lyle. Master this simple technique and the ball will pop out of the grass then roll to the hole.

Shot-Technique Tip: Select a putter; ideally a Ping-type.
Employ a very short, steep, relaxed back-stroke.

Hit down on the top quadrant of the ball, so that you impart a lively top-spin to it.

○ SHOT 76: RAINMAN PUTT

Situation: You face a forty foot lag putt. The course has just re-opened after an evening of rain, so the greens are still wet.

Strategy: Common sense tells you that adjustments are in order. However, rather than changing the tempo of your stroke, do what golfing legend Nancy Lopez showed me.

Shot-Technique Tip: At address, play the ball closer to the toe of the putter's face.

On the backswing, rotate your shoulders in a clockwise direction to promote a flatter stroke.

In swinging the putter through, rotate your right forearm clockwise so that the toe end of the club leads its heel

94

and you impart over-spin to the ball—spin that will allow you to roll the ball all the way to the hole.

○ *SHOT 77: SAVVY STROKE*

Situation: You are playing golf in midsummer and due to a lack of rain, the greens are baked out and crusty.

Strategy: You need to employ a different type of stroke.

Shot-Technique Tip: Simply make a short, shallower stroke to compensate for the super-fast rolling greens.

○ *SHOT 78: WINDY DAY PUTT*

Situation: You face a 6-foot pressure putt and the wind is blowing 30 mph.

Strategy: Sinking this putt calls for changes in your putting setup and stroke.

Shot-Technique Tip: Widen your stance when setting up, since this will help you keep your body steady. Hold the club with slightly more pressure as this will allow you to maintain good control of the putter.

Swing the club back a shorter distance than normal and through at a slightly faster speed, as I've seen Champions Tour players Andy Bean, Loren Roberts, and Jim Thorpe do while competing in tournaments.

You learn shots like this through raw experience, playing golf in different states and in various conditions.

95

SHOT 79: PUTTER-PLAY TOE-HIT

Situation: The ball rests very close to an island green, but it is against the top of a wooden piling. Therefore, you are prevented from making a normal address and swing, just as Vijay Singh once was when playing in the Tour Championship at the TPC course in Ponte Vedra, Florida.

Strategy: Think creatively, using your imagination to dream up a new shot. What follows is a figment of Vijay's imagination and a putt shot that will work wonders for you.

Shot-Technique Tip: Address the ball with your feet together, the ball played opposite your left heel, and with the toe of the putter held above the ground and pointed at the back of the ball.

Make a super-short, steep backswing, allowing your right wrist to hinge.

Hold the angle in your wrist as you bring the club into the ball, then stop so you "stun" the ball.

SHOT 80: SWEET SPOT HIT

Situation: The ball sits in uneven fringe grass, five yards from a level green and fifteen feet from the hole.

Strategy: Rather than reaching for your favorite chipping club, choose a putter. This is the high percentage play, even if the fringe grass is cut very low.

Shot-Technique Tip: Set up with the sweet spot of the putter (usually marked by club manufacturers with a dot, arrow, or line on top of the putter-head) lined up with the top of the ball.

Make a level straight-back, straight-through stroke using your arms and shoulders to control the action.

Swing the putter along the target line and toward the hole, so the putter's face contacts the top portion of the ball. This unique clubface-to-ball contact will impart over-spin to the ball and allow it to roll through the fringe toward the hole with little effect from the grass.

Greg Norman, known affectionately in golf circles as "The Shark," taught me this shot when we collaborated on an instructional series for England's *Sunday Express* newspaper.

○ *SHOT 81: FAST GREEN PUTT*

Situation: The ball is on the green, twenty feet from the hole. The bent grass common to the northeastern United States is shaved very low, so the surface is super-fast.

Strategy: In this situation, you must hit the ball at a much slower speed than you would normally from twenty feet.

Shot-Technique Tip: However, do not change your tempo. Firm up your grip then simply make a shorter back-stroke and down-stroke, as LPGA star and former *GOLF Magazine* playing editor Julie Inkster once showed me.

◯ *SHOT 82: SLOW PUTT GREEN*

Situation: The ball is on the green, twenty-five feet from the hole, but the grass is fairly long and the putting "slow."

Strategy: In this situation, you must hit the ball at a much faster speed than you would normally from this same distance, but not by speeding up the tempo of your stroke.

Shot-Technique Tip: Lighten your grip pressure, employ an extended back-stroke action, and then make a fuller, streamlined down-stroke.

> *Tailoring the Tip:* PGA Tour professional Brad Faxon is one of the best players for adapting to different conditions on the greens.

Short Game Savvy

To reach your true golfing potential, it's vital that you learn the art of getting the ball up and down when playing pitches, chips, and bunker shots from the all important sixty-yards-and-in scoring zone

I compare playing the long clubs in the bag to hitting a home run over the center field fence and playing the short clubs to laying down a soft, perfectly executed bunt into that hard-to-get-to area between the pitcher's mound and the first-base line. In short, long shots require power, short shots precision.

Pitching, chipping, and bunker play comprise the nucleus of the short game. All of these shots are played from areas close to the green, mostly with the pitching wedge,

One paramount reason why Tom Watson has won five British Open championships is a solid short game.

sand wedge, or lob wedge, and require a reasonable degree of feel or touch to achieve precision.

The three aforementioned clubs are the most lofted in a player's set of fourteen, the maximum number allowed by the Rules of Golf, and designed to lift the ball up into the air quickly so that the ball lands softly on the green. However, as you'll soon learn, low shots can be hit too, just by making simple adjustments in your setup and swing. In today's lesson, you'll also learn that certain short game situations demand using other less-lofted clubs. For example, when hitting a very long running chip, a 6-iron often works best and when faced with an extra-long bunker shot of, say, fifty yards, a 9-iron usually does the trick.

Players who can hit pitches, chips, and bunker shots close enough to the hole for an easy one-putt conversion can never be counted out of a golf match. In fact, one chief reason the European team has dominated the Americans in the Ryder Cup the last few times is because they are more versatile short game players. Granted, we have some pretty good players on our side of the Atlantic, too. Just not as many.

Pitching

In distinguishing between the standard lofted pitch and running chip, you must understand that a pitch spends more time in the air than on the ground rolling, whereas a chip flies only a short distance and rolls the rest of the way.

The pitching swing used for hitting shots from around the green is much shorter than the one used for hitting full pitches from the fairway to a hole around 100 yards away. Just how short the swing should be depends on how far you are from the spot you select for landing the ball on the green and the type of shot you want to hit; a high or low pitch.

101

Pitching experts are absolutely right to say that hitting short pitches require more finesse than force when compared with long pitches, and that hard practice is the only honest shortcut to success.

When you are prepared to devote some time to practicing pitching, structure your sessions so that you learn one new setup or swing key per day. Another good goal is to try and get to the point where you can hit more than fifty percent of your pitches within a ten-foot circle around the hole, from sixty yards out from the green, forty yards out, and twenty yards out. As you improve, keep narrowing the circle and raising your percentage-goal.

After just a few sessions, you'll be surprised how you will start matching up a particular length of shot to a particular length of swing (i.e., a half-swing or three-quarter action) and become more consistent.

Chipping

Whenever the ball sits in the fringe, a few feet off the green, you should be able to chip the ball close to the hole, provided you:

1. Analyze the lie carefully and stare at the hole until you experience yourself "feeling" the distance to the hole. (The reason you do this is to help gauge the length and strength of swing needed to propel the ball to the hole.)

2. Select a spot on the green to land the ball.
3. Select the club that will allow you to land the ball on your spot.
4. See the chip shot you intend to hit play out in your mind like a mini-movie.
5. Settle into your chipping setup, which requires you to position your feet closer together than normal and keep your hands a couple of inches ahead of the ball.
6. Rehearse the actual stroke by employing one or two practice swings.
7. Swing back smoothly, allowing your arms more than your hands to control the action.
8. Swing down, letting your hands lead the clubhead into the ball so that you hit the ball slightly on the descent.

Bunker Play

When it comes to recovering from sand, the standard short bunker play technique can be learned quickly. However, mastering the art of hitting a long bunker shot will require some hard practice. You may even want to experiment with various clubs, such as an 8-iron, 9-iron, and pitching wedge to see which works best for the distance at hand.

Whether you are playing a pitch, chip, or bunker shot, it's important to follow a set pre-swing routine that involves analyzing the lie carefully, picking the right club, and visualizing yourself employing a specific type of swing and hitting the perfect shot.

I am quick at making decisions around the greens due to the eye-hand coordination I have developed after nearly fifty years of practicing and playing golf. Playing all types of pitches, chips, and bunker shots has allowed me to store up quite a memory bank and develop an extensive repertoire. However, even though I am probably more of an expert than you at reading a short-game situation and seeing the ideal shot play out in my mind, I still take time to go over a pre-swing checklist. You must do the same or else you will not give yourself the best chance of hitting a good shot. Being too quick off the mark will mess up your score. So, before you hit a short-game shot of any kind, be confident that you have the right club in your hands and you know what to do with it.

The only further advice I can give you is to learn how to hit all of the shots contained in this chapter. Once you do, experiment by hitting shots out of different lies and dramatically changing your setup and swing, like the top professionals on the PGA, LPGA, Champions, and Nationwide Tours do. That way, you will develop new shots of your own. Remember, golf is a continuous learning process, and the more shots you have in your bag, the less

likely you are to be stumped when confronted by a unique short game lie on the golf course.

○ SHOT 83: SUPER-LOFTED SOFT-LANDING PITCH

Situation: The ball sits on a clean fairway lie, forty yards from the hole, but the line to the flagstick calls for you to carry a sand bunker and stop the ball very quickly. That's because there is only ten feet of grass between the edge of the green and the hole cut on a small level area of a se-verely sloped green.

Strategy: The ball needs to be lofted very high into the air, so that it lands extra softly. This is truly an all-or-nothing shot, requiring great concentration and vivid pre-swing imagery, so you need to really grind mentally before swinging.

Select a lob wedge, since of the three wedges in your bag this club is the most lofted.

Shot-Technique Tip: This is a shot I love to watch five-time British Open champion Tom Watson play, so I rec-ommend you use him as your model.

Set up open to the target line with a narrow stance, and put about sixty percent of your weight on your right foot. Play the ball forward in your stance and make sure your left arm and the club shaft form a straight line. Choke down on the club a couple of inches for added control. Aim the clubface directly at your target, but lay it back just slightly to increase its effective loft for even more height.

105

Swing the club back only slightly inside the target line. Rotate your left knee inward to add rhythm to your backswing's body motion.

On the downswing, rotate your right knee inward then, practically simultaneously, swing the club through thinking of putting your left hand in your left pocket. This mental image will encourage you to swing through impact fluidly, so that you slide the club underneath the ball and loft it nicely into the air.

106 Working the right knee inward like Tom Watson does here will enhance the rhythm of your swing and allow you to accelerate the club under the ball and propel it to the hole.

○ *SHOT 84: PITCH-AND-RUN*

Situation: The ball is resting atop low cut grass in the center of the fairway, fifteen yards from the front of the green and thirty yards from a hole cut on the top level of a firm two-tier green. No hazards guard the entranceway to the green, yet a strong wind is at your back.

Strategy: The prudent pro-type strategy is to hit a shot under the wind, and take advantage of the fast-running putting surface. (Because of the wind, a lofted pitch could easily get away from you and finish over the green.) Ideally, you want to hit a low shot that lands on the front of the green, bounces a couple of times, and rolls the rest of the way to the hole.

Traveling golfers should practice this shot before journeying to Scotland, the home of golf. On Scottish links courses, fairway turf is very tight and the greens very fast running. Furthermore, the greens being built nowadays are even more undulated than those on modern-day American courses. For these reasons, a lofted pitch can carom off a slope on the putting surface and finish in a deep greenside bunker. The bottom line: the pitch-and-run hit with a pitching wedge is the high percentage shot.

Shot-Technique Tip: Play the ball two inches behind your left heel and position your hands two inches ahead of the clubhead. Grip more firmly than normal to discourage active wrist action. Put slightly more weight on your left foot to promote a slight upright plane that, in turn, will allow you to bring the club down into the ball on a slight descending angle.

Swing the club back to waist height, keeping your head steady and weight left.

Swing the club down, allowing your hands to lead the clubhead into the ball. It's also vitally important that you strive for a low follow-through since this will help you make clean contact with the ball and send it flying low toward the target.

Five-time British Open champion Tom Watson gets my vote as the best ever pitch-and-run player.

⭕ *SHOT 85: SHORT DOWNHILL PITCH*

Situation: The ball lies on a downhill slope left of the green, ten yards from the putting surface and twenty yards from the hole.

Strategy: Here, the lie is so severe that you must be satisfied to land the ball on the green and keep it there. Having said that, the following setup and swing that I have observed PGA Tour pro Vijay Singh employ when competing in tournaments, could enable you to hit a super shot, provided you select a lob wedge.

Shot-Technique Tip: Position your body perpendicular to the grassy slope so that you essentially give yourself a flat lie. Set more of your weight on your right foot and keep it there from the start of the swing to its finish.

Make a long and loose backswing, allowing your right wrist to hinge.

On the downswing, swing down the slope and be sure to rotate your right hand under your left to help keep the clubface wide open and hit a high, quick-stopping shot.

One secret to success in hitting off a downhill slope, as Jack Nicklaus does here, is holding the clubface open through impact.

SHORT GAME SAVVY

○ SHOT 86: SHORT UPHILL PITCH

Situation: The ball is on the upslope in the fairway, thirty yards from a hole cut on the back of a two-tier green.

Strategy: Here you must guard against landing the ball well short of the hole. Therefore, rather than taking your lob wedge or sand wedge, select your pitching wedge.

Shot-Technique Tip: Play the ball opposite your left heel.

Swing the club back just beyond the halfway point, keeping your lower body quiet.

Swing the club down sharply into the ball, stopping at impact. This technique will allow you to impart a degree of backspin on the ball so that when it lands it will stop rather quickly.

Two-time U.S. Open champion Ernie Els, whom I once worked with on an instructional article for *GOLF Magazine*, is one of the best at playing short uphill pitch shots.

○ SHOT 87: THE SUCK-BACK WEDGE

Situation: The ball is pitching wedge distance to the hole and you face a shot to the green's top tier. The slope up to the top level of the green is very steep and there's only fifteen feet of green behind the hole.

110

Strategy: To hit the ball beyond the flag and have it "suck-back" dramatically toward the hole.

Shot-Technique Tip: Set up open with your feet narrowly spread and the ball positioned opposite your right instep. Put 70 percent of your weight on your left foot.

Swing the club up and down on a steep V-shaped arc, allowing your right arm to bend at the elbow. Be sure to begin straightening your right arm early in the downswing and drive your right shoulder downward to encourage an extra-sharp descending hit.

SHOT 88: LONG CHIP

Situation: The ball is sitting up in the fringe grass, ten feet off a level green. The distance to the hole is sixty feet.

Strategy: Because of the long distance to the hole, it is too risky to play a wedge shot. Yes, you certainly could opt to play the ball well back in your stance and hit a pitching wedge, yet I still believe the 6-iron is probably the best choice of club for handling this chipping situation.

You want the ball to carry the fringe, land on the front edge of the green, and roll all the way to the hole like a putt.

Shot-Technique Tip: Set up open to get a clear view of the hole and to help promote a much freer arm-swing. Play the ball back in your stance with your hands just ahead of the clubhead, and slightly more weight on your left foot.

111

Control the swinging action of the club by moving an imaginary triangle formed by your arms, hands, and shoulders, just like golf legend Greg Norman taught me to do.

Trigger the downswing by nudging your knees toward the target, then just rotate the triangle. Virtually automatically, the club will swing into the ball and brush the ball off the turf on a low trajectory.

◯ *SHOT 89: SHORT QUICK-STOPPING CHIP*

Situation: The ball is sitting down slightly in fringe grass, just short of the green and only fifteen feet from the hole.

A putter is out of the question, due to the so-so lie. Also, because there's little green to work with, a mid-iron is the wrong choice of club, too.

Strategy: The lob wedge is the perfect club to hit this shot with, namely because it features sixty degrees of loft build into the clubface. This club will allow you to achieve your ideal goal of hitting the ball upward quickly, so that it lands softly around a yard from the hole, bounces gently, and trickles toward the cup.

LPGA star Karrie Webb plays this shot wonderfully, so heed the following instructions based on what I learned from watching her in action on the course.

112

Shot-Technique Tip: Position the ball opposite your left heel in a narrow, open stance. Playing the ball up in your stance will encourage you to stay well behind the ball at impact, which is important to hitting a soft-landing, lob wedge shot. Setting up open will promote an out-to-in swing path that, in turn, creates left-to-right sidespin.

Swing the club back slowly with your arms and hands, while letting your wrists hinge slightly. Stop swinging back as soon as you feel weight shift to the inside of your right instep.

Swing the club gently downward, leaving most of your weight heavily on your right side. To help you slide the clubface cleanly under the ball, think of your left shoulder moving upward, your right shoulder downward, and your right hand turning under your left once the wrists straighten in the hitting area.

◯ SHOT 90: LONG BUNKER RECOVERY

Situation: The ball is sitting up in sand, twenty-five yards from the low lip of a huge bunker and another twenty-five yards from the hole.

Strategy: You must hit a low sand shot, since a ball flying on a lower trajectory will land with over-spin and run all the way to the hole. Here, the 9-iron is an ideal club to use, although I've seen Tiger Woods play this shot with an 8-iron and hit the ball close to the hole. The choice is yours.

Shot-Technique Tip: Spread your feet a couple inches wider than shoulder width and position your hands in

By keeping the majority of her weight on her right side in the hitting area, LPGA
pro Karrie Webb is aided in sending the ball flying high.

line with the ball to promote a shallow, U-shaped swing arc.

Set the club about one inch behind the ball, and hold it above the sand.

Make a three-quarter length backswing with your arms controlling the action.

Trigger the downswing by rotating your right knee inward toward your left. This knee action will increase the pulling power of your hands, so that you drive the clubhead though the sand, with the force you need to send the ball flying low and long enough.

○ *SHOT 91: SHORT BUNKER-PLAY RECOVERY*

Situation: The ball lies cleanly in a greenside bunker, ten feet from a high lip of a bunker and thirty feet from the hole.

Strategy: To loft the ball over the high bunker wall and land it close to the hole. The ideal play-club is a sand wedge, since it features fifty-six degrees of loft and a thick flange with bounce, a special design element that enables the club to slide easily through the sand and lift the ball up quickly. European tour player Colin Montgomerie plays this shot consistently well, employing the following technique.

Shot-Technique Tip: Set up open and lay the face of the club wide open.

Arm-acceleration on the downswing is critical to lofting the ball up over a high bunker lip, as Colin Montgomerie proves here.

Set the wrists early in the backswing and swing the club along your body line.

On the downswing, accelerate your arms toward the target, concentrate on slapping an area of sand about four inches behind the ball, and follow through fully.

○ *SHOT 92: BANK*

Situation: The ball you hit has finished approximately fifteen yards behind the green, at the bottom of a steep bank covered in tightly mowed grass. You're faced with a pitch to a pin cut on the back tier of a green that's well above you.

Strategy: Since the grass on the bank is manicured, play a 5-iron shot to a spot fairly low down the bank and plan on the ball skipping most of the way to the green and rolling toward the hole. (You do not want to employ a loose swing and let your wrists hinge on the backswing or else you will tend to chop down on the ball and fail to accomplish your goal.)

Shot-Technique Tip: Position the ball an inch behind your left heel in a square stance. Grip the club fairly firmly.

Swing the club back with your arms and stop the split second you feel weight shift to your right leg.

Nudge your weight toward the target, swing the club into impact with your arms, and keep the club moving low in the follow-through.

Former British Open winners Tom Watson, Seve Ballesteros, and Mark Calcavecchia all play this shot quite majestically.

Putt-Shots

Mastering golf's "ground game" and lowering your putting scores demands that you pay close attention to such variables as the degree of slope and direction of grain in greens, correctly gauge and control the speed of a putt, and learn when and how to change your setup and stroke to hit various kinds of putt-shots

The endgame of golf takes place on what's called a putting green; the last stop on a par-3, par-4, or par-5 hole.

What's so strange about this department of the game is that putting requires by far the shortest backswing and downswing in golf, yet more players struggle on the greens than anywhere else on the golf course.

According to *GOLF Magazine* surveys conducted while I worked as senior editor of instruction for that publication between 1982 and 1998, 70 percent of its two million subscribers three-putted six times per round. I'm not

Hall of Fame golfer Gary Player is one professional who has putted well throughout his career and mastered what's been called "a game within a game."

privy to present surveys, but I don't need to review them in order to know that golfers are still wasting vital strokes on the greens. This widespread problem is due largely to confusion about what method to use; lack of practice, which leads to loss of confidence; and, in the worst cases, nervous tension that causes the average club-level player to make a shaky "yip-stroke" and hit off-line putts that either fall short or finish well past the hole.

Today, there is so much misinformation about putting that even top pros test out new strokes in search of one that is easier to repeat, more reliable under pressure, and allows them to handle a variety of situations on the greens and hit sundry shots by just making some simple changes to their setup and stroke technique. In fact, Brian Lake, a very talented and low-key teaching professional, has studied the strokes of tour golfers and discovered six new unorthodox methods being employed. The trouble is, few teachers are teaching these methods, choosing only to instruct students to adopt the traditional straight-back straight-through method favored by putting guru Dave Pelz. Frankly, I use this stroke, but many other golfers have difficulty employing it, feeling they have to manipulate the club with their hands to keep the clubface square and for that reason are not consistent putters.

Whatever stroke you choose to employ—after taking lessons from your club pro or experimenting with different methods on the practice putting green—you will face sundry shot-making situations on the greens during a round of golf, so let me help you increase your knowledge by offering unique shot-technique putting tips.

○ SHOT 93: LONG PUTT

Situation: You face a fifty-foot putt on a level, fast green.

Strategy: Concentrate on lagging the ball up close to the hole and if it rolls in consider that a bonus. Two putts is a very good putting score from fifty feet, so do not charge the hole. Try to "die" the ball to the hole.

Shot-Technique Tip: Set up slightly closed, with your right foot dropped back further slightly from the target line than your left foot. Position the ball opposite your left heel and grip more lightly with your natural right hand since it is considered the hand that controls the speed of a putt.

Tailoring the Tip: Women golfers should observe the putting stroke of Christie Kerr, whom I think is the LPGA's best lag-putter.

Swing the putter back slightly inside the target line and make a longer stroke than normal, but keep your tempo the same. Rotate your shoulders in a counterclockwise direction to help you square the putter face up at impact and swing it back to the inside after the ball is struck.

Ben Crenshaw, winner of the Masters in 1984 and 1995, is unquestionably the best long-putter of all time.

◯ *SHOT 94: SHORT PRESSURE PUTT*

Situation: You face a dead-straight three-foot "knee-knocker" to win the match.

Strategy: Stroke the ball firmly into the cup.

Shot-Technique Tip: Set up square, with your feet, knees, hips, and shoulders parallel to the ball-hole target line. Grip the club more firmly to help promote a square-to-square putting action. Aim the putter's face directly at the hole.

Swing the putter back low along the target line. Allow your left shoulder to rotate downward and your right shoulder to rise up. This seesaw action will further ensure that the putter stays square to the hole.

Rock your shoulders in the opposite manner, to ensure a straight-through stroke and a square, on-line hit.

Jack Nicklaus, in my opinion, is the best short-putter of all time.

◯ *SHOT 95: TEN FOOT POP-STROKE*

Situation: You face a dead-straight putt of ten feet on a medium-speed green, a surface that is between fast and slow.

Strategy: Do what legendary golfer and multiple major championship winner Gary Player has done throughout

One non-technical reason why Jack Nicklaus holed so many short pressure putts during his long career was his unique ability to correctly "read" subtle breaks in a green and "see" the ball fall into the cup before he putted, which raised his level of confidence—and will yours!

his career: "pop" the ball with the putter. Having worked on instructional articles with Gary, let me explain his secrets to success.

Shot-Technique Tip: Set up square with your elbows resting on your hips.

On the back-stroke, let your right wrist hinge slightly as you swing the putter back on a line square to the hole.

On the down-stroke, re-hinge your right wrist so that the putter head springs into impact and you kind of pop the ball with the putter's face. This little secret of Gary's adds acceleration to the club in the impact zone and helps you propel the ball dead-on-line into the cup.

○ *SHOT 96: DOWN-GRAIN PUTT*

Situation: You face a twenty-foot putt. The grassy line leading from the ball to the hole has a shiny glow to it, signaling a faster down-grain putt.

Strategy: You must "deaden" the hit.

Shot-Technique Tip: Address the ball off the toe of the putter.

Employ your normal back-stroke for a twenty-foot putt.

Hit the ball with the toe of the putter rather than the sweet spot of the putter's

> *Tailoring the Tip:* Nick Faldo, now a television golf commentator for NBC, is also regarded as one of the best at reading grain in greens. And rightfully so, considering the Englishman has won golf tournaments all over the world on different putting surfaces.

125

Golfing great Gary Player poised in the address position, all setup to hit a pop-stroke putt. Look and learn.

face. This will deaden the hit and compensate for the slick putting surface.

Golfing legend Billy Casper, whom I once worked with on a putting article, is regarded by many golf experts and professionals as the best down-grain, up-grain putter ever.

○ *SHOT 97: UP-GRAIN PUTT*

Situation: You face a twenty-foot putt. The grassy line leading from the ball to the hole has a dull look to it, signaling a slower, up-grain putt.

Strategy: You must "liven" the hit.

Shot-Technique Tip: Address the ball and swing the putter the same way you normally would for this length putt. However, on the downswing concentrate on hitting the top half of the ball to impart lively over-spin on the ball and compensate for the slower surface.

○ *SHOT 98: RIGHT-TO-LEFT BREAKING PUTT*

Situation: You face a fifteen-foot putt that breaks six inches from right to left on a fairly fast green.

Strategy: Keep the ball rolling on the right or "high" side of the hole until it reaches the crest of the break. At that point it should start breaking or turning down toward the hole. Concentrate on more of a die-stroke than a charge-the-hole stroke.

127

Shot-Technique Tip: Aim the putter-face six inches to the right of the hole. Set your feet and body square to that spot. Play the ball farther back in your stance than you would normally on a level putt.

Swing the putter back freely with your arms and shoulders, so it stays square to your aiming point.

Swing the putter through with your arms and shoulders, keeping the putter moving at your aiming point, just like I've observed teenage sensation Michelle Wie do well when she's in the zone.

No golfer beats Bob Charles at hitting good breaking putts. At *GOLF Magazine* I worked with Bob and, quite shockingly, he holed practically every right-to-left and left-to-right breaking putt he faced.

○ ### *SHOT 99: LEFT-TO-RIGHT BREAKING PUTT*

Situation: You face a fifteen-foot putt that breaks six inches from left to right on a fairly fast green.

Strategy: Keep the ball rolling on the left or "low side" until it reaches the crest of the break. At that point it should start curving down toward the hole. Favor the die-stroke over the charge-the-hole stroke.

Shot-Technique Tip: Aim the putter-face six inches to the left of the hole. Set your feet and body square to that aiming point. Play the ball forward in your stance to en-

128

courage the putter-face to contact the ball as it's almost closing and you'll keep the ball on the high side.

Swing the putter back freely with your arms and shoulders, so it stays square to your aiming point.

Swing the putter through with your arms and shoulders, keeping the putter moving at your aiming point.

○ *SHOT 100: DOWNHILL CUT-PUTT*

Situation: You face a thirty-foot putt from a flat area of green down a steep slope to a hole below.

Strategy: Repeat the buzz words "slow pace" a few times while preparing to putt. In short, you must hit the ball at a much slower speed so that it dies as it nears the hole.

Shot-Technique Tip: Set up open, swing the putter back outside the target line, and swing down and through, across the target line to impart a slight degree of cut-spin on the ball. To this day, I've never seen any pro golfer hit this type of putt better than Hall of Fame player Lee Trevino.

○ *SHOT 101: UPHILL HOOK-PUTT*

Situation: The ball is at the bottom of a slope on the green, and you are hitting to a hole cut on the top level of a medium-pace green.

Strategy: It helps to imagine a second golf hole a couple of feet beyond the "real" one, but that's not enough to en-

129

sure that you hit the ball the proper distance. The answer is to set up and swing the putter the way teacher Phil Ritson told me his fellow South African and golf legend Bobby Locke once did.

Shot-Technique Tip: Set up closed, with imaginary lines running across your feet, knees, hips, and shoulders pointing right of target.

Swing the putter back on a very flat path, rotating your forearms clockwise and opening the putter-face.

Rotate your forearms in the opposite direction to close the putter's face at impact and impart controlled hook-spin to the ball. This added spin will cause the ball to roll nicely to the hole.

In observing Champions Tour players, I've noticed Jays Haas employs a similar method to Locke.

Acknowledgments

My editor, Mark Weinstein, came up with the idea to write this book. I'm grateful to Mark, an editor I respect highly and really enjoy working with.

Thanks also go out to Tony Lyons, Skyhorse's publisher, for believing in this project and having faith in me to write it.

I'm also deeply indebted to *Golfweek* magazine. This fine publication, known best for golf-news scoops, agreed to run excerpts from this book which I'm sure will please readers looking to lower their handicaps.

I owe thanks, too, to Bill Robertson, my former editor at *Golf Illustrated* magazine in London, and George

Peper, my former editor at *GOLF Magazine* in New York City. These two passionate golfers opened the door for me to enter the world of professional golf and sent me on the road to work on instructional articles with the game's best tour golfers and top teachers on both sides of the Atlantic. Much of what I learned during my travels interviewing and observing players can be found in this book, along with my own shot-making tips based on fifty years of personal playing experience.

Lastly, I'm grateful to Yasuhiro Tanabe, whose wonderfully vivid photographs enhance the visual flavor of Golfweek's *101 Winning Golf Tips* and help to clearly relay my instructional messages.

List of Shots

Chapter 1: Driving the Ball

- Shot 1: Dead-Straight Power-Play
- Shot 2: Super-Controlled Power-Slice
- Shot 3: Super-Controlled Power-Hook
- Shot 4: Ride the Wind Tee-Ball
- Shot 5: Wind Cheater
- Shot 6: Super-Controlled Draw-Play
- Shot 7: Three-Metal-Fade
- Shot 8: Super-Hot Two-Iron Stinger

Chapter 2: Par-3 Tee Shots

- Shot 9: One-Iron Laser
- Shot 10: Three-Metal Rocket
- Shot 11: Left-to-Right Crosswind Control-Play
- Shot 12: Right-to-Left Crosswind Control-Play
- Shot 13: Mid-Iron Back-Up
- Shot 14: Mid-Iron "Releaser"
- Shot 15: Hit-to-Hell Tee Ball
- Shot 16: Hit-to-Heaven Tee Ball

Chapter 3: Fairway Plays

- Shot 17: Driver-off-the-Deck Long Approach
- Shot 18: Down-Under Fairway-Metal-Play
- Shot 19: Iron "High Ball"
- Shot 20: Long Iron "Runner"
- Shot 21: Ball-Above-Feet Sidehill Recovery-Play
- Shot 22: Ball-Below-Feet Sidehill Recovery-Play
- Shot 23: Uphill Iron Approach
- Shot 24: Downhill Iron Approach

SHOTS

Chapter 5: Short Game Savvy

Chapter 6: Putt-Shots